OCR

British depth study 1906–1918

BRITISH SOCIETY IN CHANGE

COLIN SHEPHARD

ROSEMARY REES

JOHN MURRAY

Mark schemes

Mark schemes for the Source Investigations in Part 2 can be downloaded free of charge from www.johnmurray.co.uk or obtained from the marketing department at the address below.
Telephone 020 7493 4361
e-mail promo@johnmurrays.co.uk

First published in 2002
by John Murray (Publishers) Ltd
50 Albemarle Street
London W1S 4BD

Layouts by Black Dog Design
Artwork by Mike Humphries, Janek Matysiak

Typeset in 11/12 pt Bodoni Book by Servis Filmsetting Ltd, Manchester
Printed and bound in Spain by Bookprint, S.L., Barcelona

A catalogue entry for this title is available from the British Library

ISBN 0 7195 7734 9

Contents

Acknowledgements   iv

Introduction: using historical sources   1

Part 1   What happened 1906–1918?   **5**

What was Britain like at the beginning of the twentieth century? 6

1 The reforms of the Liberal Government 1906–1912   8

2 Votes for women   22

3 Britain during the First World War   53

Part 2   Source investigations   **73**

1 Why did the Liberal Government (1906–1912) decide to
      fight poverty?   74

2 How important were the Liberal social reforms?   77

3 Were the suffragettes justified in using violence?   80

4 Was Emily Davison exploited by the suffragettes?   83

5 Women's war work: What did it achieve for women?   86

6 Did the First World War help or hinder women getting
      the vote?   89

7 How effective was government propaganda during the
      First World War?   93

Index   **98**

ACKNOWLEDGEMENTS

The Publishers would like to thank the following for permission to reproduce copyright material:

Photo credits

Cover *l–r* MEPL, Hulton Archive, Punch; **p.2** Museum of London; **p.5** Imperial War Museum; **p.6** *l* Corbis, *r* Beamish Open Air Museum, *b* Liverpool City Council; **p.7** *tl* Hulton Archive, *tr* Topham Picturepoint, *bl* Science & Society Picture Library, *br* Oldham Local Studies & Archive; **p.9** Mary Evans Picture Library; **p.10** *t* Mary Evans Picture Library, *b* Salvation Army International Heritage Centre; **p.11** Cambridge County & Folk Museum; **p.12** *both* Hulton Archive; **p.13** Topham Picturepoint; **p.14** Hulton Archive; **p.16** London Metropolitan Archives; **p.18** Suffolk Record Office; **p.20** Punch; **p.23** *t* London Metropolitan Archives, *b* British Telecom; **p.24** *both* Hulton Archive; **p.27** Museum of London; **p.28** Mary Evans Picture Library; **p.29** Punch; **p.32** *t* Museum of London, *b* Mary Evans Picture Library; **p.33** *t* Mary Evans Picture Library, *b* Museum of London; **p.34** Mary Evans Picture Library; **p.35** Museum of London; **p.38** *t* Topham Picturepoint, *b* Museum of London; **p.39** *t* Museum of London, *b* Hulton Archive; **p.40** Museum of London; **p.41** Museum of London; **p.42** Museum of London; **p.43** Hulton Archive; **p.49** Museum of London; **p.50** Hulton Archive; **p.53** Imperial War Museum; **p.54** St Helens Public Library; **p.55** *all* Imperial War Museum; **p.57** Imperial War Museum; **p.58** Lincolnshire Archives Office; **p.59** Punch; **p.60** *both* Imperial War Museum; **p.61** Imperial War Museum; **p.62** *both* Imperial War Museum; **p.63** Imperial War Museum; **p.64** *both* Imperial War Museum; **p.65** *tl* Imperial War Museum, *cl* Museum of London, *bl* Topham Picturepoint, *tr, br* Imperial War Museum; **p.66** Imperial War Museum; **p.67** Imperial War Museum; **p.68** Imperial War Museum; **p.70** *all* Imperial War Museum *except br* Punch; **p.71** Imperial War Museum; **p.72** *all* Imperial War Museum; **p.73** Museum of London; **p.74** Liverpool Records Office; **p.75** *l* Liberal Democrats/University of Bristol Archives, *r* Hulton Archive; **p.76** Punch; **p.78** *t, bl* Punch, *br* Museum of London; **p.80** Museum of London; **p.81** *both* Museum of London; **p.83** British Library Newspaper Archives; **p.84** Hulton Archive; **p.85** Centre for Study of Cartoons and Caricature/Mirror Syndication; **p.86** Imperial War Museum; **p.87** *both* Imperial War Museum; **p.90** Museum of London; **p.91** Museum of London; **p.93** *both* Imperial War Museum; **p.94** *both* Imperial War Museum; **p.95** *t* Topham Picturepoint, *b* Press Association; **p.96** *both* Imperial War Museum.

t = top, *b* = bottom, *l* = left, *r* = right, *c* = centre.

Written sources

p.4 *The Lancet*, 1912; **p.9** *Poverty: A study of town life* by Benjamin Seebohm Rowntree, Policy Press, 2000; **p.10** *People of the Abyss* by Jack London, Pluto Press, 2001; **p.13** *Life and Labour of the People in London* by Charles Booth, 1889–1903; **p.21** Source 16: *The Liberals in Power* by C Cross, 1963, Source 17: *The Origins of the Liberal Welfare State* by J R Hay, Palgrave, 1983; **p.27** *The Great Scourge and How to end it* by Christabel Pankhurst, 1913; **p.35** *My Own Story* by Emmeline Pankhurst, Greenwood Press, 1985; **p.43** *The Lancet*, 1912; **p.44** Extract from *Unshackled: The Story of How We Won the Vote* by Christabel Pankhurst, published by Hutchinson. Used by permission of the Random House Group; **p.48** Source 50: Extract from *Unshackled: The Story of How We Won the Vote* by Christabel Pankhurst, published by Hutchinson. Used by permission of the Random House Group, Source 51: *Rise Up, Women!* by Andrew Rosen, Gregg Revivals, 1993; **p.56** *The First Day on the Somme* by Martin Middlebrook, Penguin Books, 2001; **p.74** *Round About a Pound a Week* by Maud Pember Reeves, Virago, 1988; **p.77** Source B: *Lark Rise to Candleford* by Flora Thompson, 1945, by permission of Oxford University Press, Source C: *The Classic Slum* by Richard Roberts, Manchester University Press, 1973; **p.78** *Tomorrow is a New Day* by Jennie Lee, 1939; **p.80** Source A: Extract from *Unshackled: The Story of How We Won the Vote* by Christabel Pankhurst, published by Hutchinson. Used by permission of the Random House Group, Source B: *My Own Story* by Emmeline Pankhurst, Greenwood Press, 1985; **p.82** Source I: *The Strange Death of Liberal England* by George Dangerfield, Stanford University Press, 1997, Source K: *The March of the Women* by Martin Pugh, 2000, by permission of Oxford University Press; **p.84** Source C: *The Suffrage Movement: An Intimate Account of Persons and Ideals* by Sylvia Pankhurst, 1931, Source E: Extract from *Unshackled: The Story of How We Won the Vote* by Christabel Pankhurst, published by Hutchinson. Used by permission of the Random House Group, Source G: *The Emancipation of Women* by D C Brooks, 1970; **p.88** *Women's Weekly*, 1918; **p.89** *The March of the Women* by Martin Pugh, 2000, by permission of Oxford University Press; **p.90** Source D: Extract from *Unshackled: The Story of How We Won the Vote* by Christabel Pankhurst, published by Hutchinson. Used by permission of the Random House Group, Source E: *The March of the Women* by Martin Pugh, 2000, by permission of Oxford University Press; **p.94** Source D: *Blighty: British Society in the Era of the Great War* by G J Degroot, Longman (Pearson Education), 1996, Source F: *Poor Bloody Volunteers* by W H A Groom, Source G: *With a Machine Gun to Cambrai* by George Coppard, Cassell Military, 1999.

Every effort has been made to trace all copyright holders, but if any have been inadvertently overlooked the Publishers will be pleased to make the necessary arrangements at the first opportunity.

Introduction: using historical sources

If you are using this book then you will be preparing for a GCSE examination paper on British Society in Change 1906–18.

This examination paper will consist of a source investigation on an issue taken from one of the following three themes:

- The Liberal reforms 1906–12
- Votes for women 1900–18
- The Home Front 1914–18.

The examination paper will test your ability to understand, evaluate and use historical sources. There will be six or seven questions.

Although the paper is mainly a test of your source skills, to gain high marks you will need to use your knowledge of the topic as well. This book is designed:

- to tell you what you need to know about British society 1906–18 (Part 1)
- to give you plenty of practice in developing your source investigation skills (Part 2).

HANDY HINTS

Some handy hints in answering the exam questions:

1. All the questions in the exam will be about sources – make sure you use them in all your answers. Never write an answer that makes no use of the sources.

2. Do not write too much in answer to the earlier questions. If a question is worth 6 marks, you will never score more than 6 marks even if you write 19 pages! Answer the question, then move on. Do not try to impress the examiner by writing everything you know about the topic. What they want is an answer to the question.

3. When you are using evidence from sources always make clear to the examiner which source you are using.

4. Always support your answer with examples and explanations.

5. Remember – there are no 'right' answers. The examiner is looking for intelligent answers that are supported by the sources and by your knowledge. Lots of different answers will all be given top marks because they are intelligent answers.

6. Sometimes it will be a good idea to use sources in your answer which are not mentioned in the question. Only do this if it helps you write a better answer. For example, if a question asks you how reliable a source is, one of the other sources in the paper might throw some light on this by contradicting the first source.

7. How do you use your knowledge of the topic? This is a tricky one. The golden rule is only use knowledge if it helps you say something better about the sources mentioned in the question. Your knowledge could be used to help you:
   - explain the meaning of a source
   - explain the possible purpose of a source, or suggest who might have written or drawn the source
   - decide if a source is reliable
   - check what the source says against what you know about the events
   - look at who wrote the source – you might know something about them which will help you decide if the source is reliable.

8. The final question on the paper will ask you to reach a conclusion about the issue under investigation. Make sure you base your answer on the sources. Remember, the sources will always support two different viewpoints. Make sure you explain how some sources support one viewpoint, then show how other sources support the other viewpoint. Also, say something about how reliable some of the sources are – this will help you reach a conclusion about which viewpoint the sources support the most.

How to use sources

In the exam you might come across three types of sources:

1 **Written sources**
   These might be first-hand accounts, memoirs, newspaper articles, extracts from history books etc.
2 **Pictorial sources**
   These might be paintings, cartoons, photographs etc.
3 **Statistical sources**
   These will be tables or graphs of figures.

Never try to reach a judgement about a source based simply on what type of source it is. Knowing that a source is an eyewitness account, a photograph or from a memoir does not, in itself, tell you if the source is useful or reliable.

- Do *not* say it is reliable because it is a photograph
- Do *not* say it is unreliable because it was written much later
- Do *not* say it is reliable because the person saw what happened.

Answering source-based questions

● **SOURCE A**

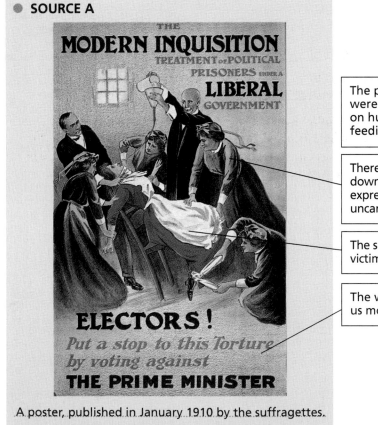

The poster was issued by the suffragettes who were being force-fed in prison when they were on hunger strike. They wanted the force-feeding to be stopped.

There are five people holding the suffragette down – this makes it look brutal and unfair. The expressions on their faces make them look uncaring.

The suffragette has been drawn as a helpless victim to make people sympathise with her.

The words used on the poster like 'torture' give us more clues.

A poster, published in January 1910 by the suffragettes.

1 Why was this poster published in 1910?

Study the source
The first thing to do is to work out the message of the poster. The notes in the boxes will give you some guidance. Ask yourself, what is happening in the poster? Look at the poster and use your knowledge – a suffragette prisoner is being force-fed.

Then ask, does the artist approve or disapprove of the force-feeding? What are the clues that help answer this?

Now to the question – 'Why was this poster published in 1910?'
We have already worked out enough to write quite a good answer. The poster was published to show people how terrible force-feeding was.

You have probably already thought of a way of developing this answer. The poster was published to get people to oppose force-feeding and to put pressure on the Government to stop it. (You will need to support these claims by using the details in the poster and your knowledge.)

However, there is one more step. The question asked 'Why was this poster published in 1910?'

After you have studied this topic you will know that the Liberal Government held an election in January 1910. The suffragettes published this poster to encourage people to vote against the Government because it supported force-feeding. (See the clues about this at the bottom of the poster.) The suffragettes hoped that this would put pressure on the Government to stop force-feeding.

Task
Look at the answer below.

1 What are its strengths?
2 How could it be improved?

This poster was published to make people see how dreadful force-feeding was. Force-feeding was used on the suffragettes when they went on hunger strike. The prison authorities could not let the women die so they had them fed like it shows in the picture. This has been drawn to make it look really horrible and to get people to oppose it.

● **SOURCE B**

People were held down by force, flung on to the floor, tied to chairs and iron bedsteads while the tube was forced up the nostrils. After each feeding the nasal pain gets worse. The wardress endeavoured to make one prisoner open her mouth by sawing the edge of a cup along the gums. The broken edge caused laceration and severe pain. Food into the lung of one unresisting prisoner immediately caused severe choking, vomiting and persistent coughing. She was hurriedly released next day suffering from pneumonia and pleurisy. We cannot believe that any of our colleagues will agree that this form of prison treatment is justly described in Mr McKenna's words as necessary medical treatment.

From the medical journal *The Lancet*, August 1912.
The Lancet is published by doctors, for doctors.

2 Which source gives more reliable evidence about force-feeding, Source A or Source B?

This question is about reliability: be careful not to make unsupported assertions based on who wrote or drew the source. For example, 'Source B is more reliable because doctors do not lie. The suffragettes are biased in Source A and they cannot be trusted', would not get many marks. Another answer to avoid is one that only uses the content of the sources. For example, 'Source B is more reliable – it tells me a lot more about force-feeding.' This is nonsense – a source is not more reliable just because it contains more information.

One thing you have probably noticed about these two sources is that they do agree about details – suffragettes being held down and the tube being forced up the nostrils. You could claim that this means both sources are reliable. This would get you some marks, but for the top marks you need to think harder.

When you are asked about the reliability of a source, it is important to:

• think carefully about the purpose of the source
• compare what the source is claiming with your own knowledge.

Source A, as you have seen, was trying to get force-feeding stopped. It aimed to influence people, which means it is biased.

Source B is probably more trustworthy. It was written by doctors who would know what was happening during force-feeding because it was supervised in the prison. The writers are obviously horrified by the practice, but this is a genuine reaction to the horror they have seen. The fact that they are writing in a medical journal is also important – they do not have a wider political purpose like the creators of Source A.

When you come to questions like this in the exam, you will know quite a bit about topics like force-feeding. This means you can check what the sources are claiming against what you know. You will know details that will support both sources. Use this knowledge. However, be careful – it can also be argued that:

• Force-feeding was necessary to stop the hunger strikers from dying.
• Many middle- and upper-class suffragettes were released from prison as soon as they went on hunger strike, so force-feeding was not used on all women.

There are no 'right' answers to this kind of question. The ideas above suggest that Source B is the more reliable, but this does not mean that Source A is totally unreliable or that there are no doubts about Source B.

Task

Look at the answer below. See if you can complete the sections that have been left blank.

I think that Source B is more reliable than Source A. Source A was published by the suffragettes. They were against force-feeding because ...

The artist of the poster had deliberately made force-feeding look dreadful by ...

The suffragettes had a purpose in publishing this poster. They were trying to ...

Source B, on the other hand, is more reliable. There are several reasons for this ...

However, I do have some doubts about Source B because ...

Overall, I think ... is the more reliable source.

Part 1
What happened 1906–1918?

What was Britain like at the beginning of the twentieth century?

At the beginning of the twentieth century Britain was a country of contrasts: of rich and poor, town and country, North and South. It was a country where faster communications and increasing wealth were creating a society where traditional boundaries were becoming blurred. The upper classes could no longer expect automatic respect from those whose lives they controlled. More and more women were unwilling to fit into the image of obedient wife and mother. Working people, both men and women, were expecting to be involved in decisions that affected their lives at work and at home.

● **SOURCE 1**

Society women were considered beautiful only if they had 'hour-glass' figures. They needed tightly-laced corsets if they were to achieve the figure of Camille Gifford, the woman in this photograph. Some manufacturers, like the one in the advertisement, cashed in on this fashion and produced electrically-powered corsets.

● **SOURCE 2**

A photograph of a busy street corner in Liverpool, 1908.

● **SOURCE 3**

A London slum photographed in 1909.

● **SOURCE 4**

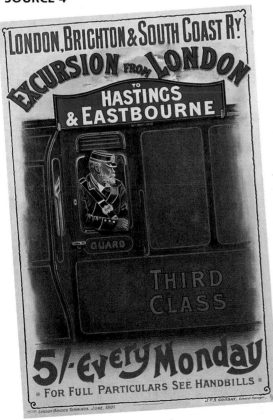

By 1900, a rail network covered the country. Goods and people were carried quickly, efficiently and cheaply, and thousands of people could afford a seaside holiday. This poster is advertising cheap excursions to Hastings and Eastbourne on the south coast.

● **SOURCE 5**

A photograph of 'The Stores' in Fore Street, Taunton in 1904. Some shopkeepers changed from selling just a few items to selling many different products. The aim was to attract better-off customers who wanted to see a wide range of goods under one roof. These shops were called department stores and were found in market towns, like this one, as well as in big cities.

● **SOURCE 6**

These spinners in a Lancashire cotton mill were photographed in 1910. They are changing the bobbins of thread on the spinning machine behind them.

The reforms of the Liberal Government 1906–12

The turn of the century

On 22 January 1901, Britain was plunged into mourning. Flags flew at half-mast; church bells tolled; children were forbidden to play; people closed their blinds and curtains and, if they could, dressed in black. Queen Victoria had died after a reign of just over 63 years. Not many people could remember a time when she hadn't been their monarch. Her death, coming almost at the turn of the century, seemed to many people to be symbolic of the ending of an era and to herald the dawn of a new one.

The Victorians had achieved a great deal:

- Hours of work had been steadily reduced and work conditions improved in shops, offices, mines, factories and mills.
- Slum clearance schemes were well under way and most houses had piped water and lavatories that were connected to a sewerage system.
- All children had to go to school.
- All male householders had the right to vote.
- Wages had risen and the average family was better off at the end of Queen Victoria's reign than it had been at the beginning.

All these improvements formed a basis for hope and a belief that things would get better. However, the Victorians had left many problems unsolved and perhaps the biggest one was the problem of poverty.

What was it like to be poor at the beginning of the twentieth century?

The poor had to depend on private charities or on the state-established system of poor relief for help in bad times.

Charities

Private charities gave help in the form of money, clothes or food. Sometimes they provided accommodation for the elderly and destitute. By 1905, there were 700–800 private charities operating in London alone. In towns and cities throughout Britain there were thousands of abandoned children. They lived on the streets by begging and thieving, and many of them died from starvation, disease and neglect. Some charities dealt specially with children. Dr Thomas Barnardo started one such charity in 1867. By 1905, when he died, Dr Barnardo had set up a network of children's homes across the country. He had rescued some 59,384 children from destitution and helped around 500,000 to lead better lives.

The Poor Law

The most dreaded and feared type of help, however, was that provided by the State through the Poor Law. Workhouses provided food and shelter for the poor. They were grim places. Conditions were awful. The usual form of relief, however, was outdoor relief (meaning outside the workhouse): payments sometimes in cash and sometimes in goods or services, to people in their own homes. It was one thing to be poor, but quite another to accept relief. This meant being labelled a 'pauper' and tremendous shame and disgrace was attached to this.

Most Victorians believed that the poor were somehow responsible for their own poverty, but by the beginning of the twentieth century, people were beginning to see that there were social and economic reasons for poverty, and that it was not always the fault of the poor themselves. Amongst the poor there was a deeply ingrained dread of the workhouse and of accepting any kind of relief attached to the Poor Law. To accept relief was to give up responsibility for yourself and your family; it was to admit defeat.

Men and women were expected to save from their wages so that they had enough money to help them through bad times. Few poor people could do this and so most dreaded sickness and unemployment. Above all, they dreaded retirement, when they were too old to work. Unless they had relatives, willing and able to look after them, the poor faced a miserable old age. For millions of people in Britain, the dawn of the twentieth century brought no obvious hope of better times.

● **SOURCE 1**

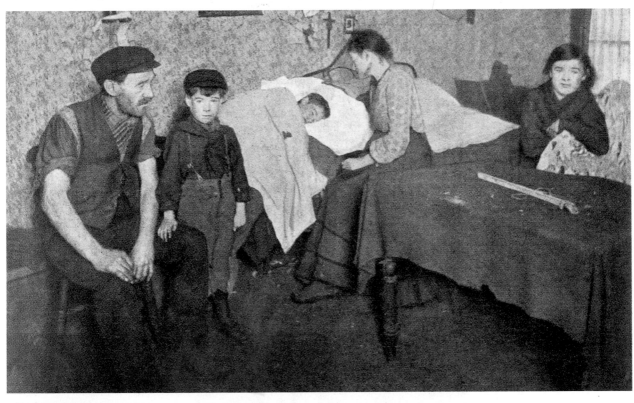

A photograph of a poor family, living in one room, at the beginning of the twentieth century.

● **SOURCE 2**

They must never purchase a halfpenny newspaper or spend a penny to buy a ticket for a popular concert. They must never contribute anything to their church or chapel, or give help to a neighbour which costs them money. They cannot save, nor can they join a sick club or a Trade Union, because they cannot afford the contributions. The children must have no pocket money for dolls, marbles or sweets. The father must smoke no tobacco and must drink no beer. The mother must never buy any pretty clothes for herself or her children. The wage earner must never be absent from his work for a single day.

Seebohm Rowntree investigated poverty in York. In his book, *Poverty: a Study of Town Life*, published in 1901, he described the pressures on a poor family.

● **SOURCE 3**

A photograph of boys in a school playground, taken around 1910. It was used by George Sims in his series of books, *Living London*, which he wrote to show different sorts of poverty in the capital city.

● **SOURCE 4**

The members of a poor family cannot ride in buses or trams, cannot write letters, take outings, go to social or benefit clubs, nor can they buy sweetmeats, tobacco, books or newspapers. And further, should one child require a pair of shoes, the family must not eat meat for a week in order to pay for them.

Jack London was an American journalist who travelled the world looking for good stories. In his book, *People of the Abyss*, he described the way the poor lived in London before 1914.

● **SOURCE 5**

This photograph was taken for the Salvation Army in the early 1900s. They used it as part of their campaign to raise money for the poor. This mother and her four children have probably been to a soup kitchen – they have enamel bowls, a mug and thick slices of bread in front of them.

● **SOURCE 6**

The women's day-room in the Cambridge workhouse, photographed in 1880.
As the twentieth century approached, workhouses were less grim than they had
been earlier in the nineteenth century. Attitudes were beginning to change.
However, many old people still lived in fear of having to go into a workhouse.

Task

1 Look at Source 1 and read Source 2 on page 9. Which source gives the most
   reliable impression of life for the poor at the beginning of the twentieth
   century? Give reasons for your answer.
2 Now look at Sources 3, 5 and 6. Which photograph gives the most useful
   image of life for the poor in early twentieth-century Britain?
3 Using all the sources, write down ten words that best describe what life was
   like for the poor at the beginning of the twentieth century.

Why did poverty come to the public's attention at the turn of the century?

Poverty came to the public's attention at the end of the nineteenth and beginning of the twentieth centuries, partly because of surveys and investigations run by individuals and organisations, and partly because of the charity work done by men and women who were concerned about the condition of the poor.

The Salvation Army

Many Christian groups ran missions in the inner cities where they preached the word of God, hoping to turn prostitutes and petty criminals away from 'sin'. Some of them gave away hot soup and bread, too. William and Catherine Booth went one step further. Instead of waiting for the poor to come to them at their mission in East London, they went to the poor wherever they could find them: on street corners and in pubs, living rough on park benches and under the embankment arches. Their East London mission expanded until, in 1878, it had around 45 branches and was called the Salvation Army. Organised rather like an army, with William Booth as the 'general' and full-time workers called majors and captains, the Salvation Army used attention-grabbing techniques, like smart uniforms and brass bands, to attract the crowds and bring in the money. By 1900, the Salvation Army was running its own training centres, a labour exchange to help people find jobs, a farm and a brickworks. All these were designed to employ and train the poor, to give them a sense of purpose and to help them lead useful lives.

The Salvation Army officers gathered a great deal of information about the poor and about the causes of poverty. This showed that some of the causes of poverty were beyond the control of ordinary people. It was not their fault they were poor. William Booth understood this. He described poverty and the poor in terms of three circles.

William Booth 1829–1912

Catherine Booth 1829–90

● **SOURCE 7**

The outer and widest circle was inhabited by 'the starving and homeless but honest poor'.

Next came the circle inhabited by 'those who live by vice'.

In the centre were 'those who live by crime'.

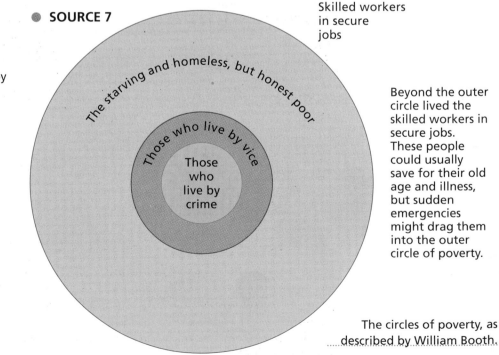

Skilled workers in secure jobs

The starving and homeless, but honest poor

Those who live by vice

Those who live by crime

Beyond the outer circle lived the skilled workers in secure jobs. These people could usually save for their old age and illness, but sudden emergencies might drag them into the outer circle of poverty.

The circles of poverty, as described by William Booth.

Charles Booth (1840–1916)

Charles Booth (no relation to William and Catherine Booth) was born into a wealthy Liverpool ship-owning family and in the mid-1870s, he moved the company offices to London. He refused to accept the official statistics that said that about 25 per cent of the working population was living in poverty. He decided to find out for himself and set up his own team of paid investigators. Over a period of around 17 years (1886–1903) he and his team investigated the living conditions, income and spending of over 4000 people and reported their findings on a regular basis. These were published between 1889 and 1903 in 17 volumes, called *Life and Labour of the People in London*.

Charles Booth found that nearly 31 per cent of Londoners were living below what he called the 'poverty line'. By this, he meant that they did not have the money to buy enough food, shelter and clothing. He divided the poor into four groups:

● **SOURCE 8**

Class A

The lowest class: street-sellers, criminals, loafers. Their life is the life of savages with extreme hardship.
11,000 or 1.25% of the poor.

Class B

Casual earnings: widows and deserted women; part-time labourers; many shiftless and helpless.
110,000 or 11.25% of the poor.

Class C

Occasional earnings: hit by trade depressions.
75,000 or 8% of the poor.

Class D

Low wages: less than 21 [shillings] a week; wages barely enough to stay alive. Includes dock labourers and gas workers.
129,000 or 14.5% of the poor.

From Charles Booth, *Life and Labour of the People in London*, 1889–1903.

Perhaps more importantly, Booth worked out that 85 per cent of people living in poverty were poor because of problems relating to unemployment and low wages. In other words, poverty wasn't their own fault, as so many Victorians had believed.

All this was true for London, but maybe London wasn't typical. What about other big cities?

Seebohm Rowntree (1871–1954)

Benjamin Seebohm Rowntree belonged to the family of York-based chocolate manufacturers. The family were Quakers and their principles led them to treat their workers well, by the standards of the time. Rowntree was particularly interested in Charles Booth's findings about the London poor and wanted to see whether what he had discovered was also true of poor people in York.

He calculated that a family of five (two parents and three children) could live on 21s (shillings) 8d (pence) a week. Using this as his baseline, he found that around 28 per cent of the population of York were living in poverty. He divided this poverty into two kinds:

- **Primary poverty:** No matter how hard a family worked, they would never earn enough to provide themselves with adequate food, shelter and clothing. These families didn't stand a chance.
- **Secondary poverty:** These families could just about feed, clothe and shelter themselves, provided there were no additional calls on their income. These families were living on the edge.

About 10 per cent of the people of York were living in primary poverty and around 18 per cent in secondary poverty. Rowntree then drew on Booth's idea of a poverty line and worked out when individuals might find themselves above or below this line.

● **SOURCE 9**

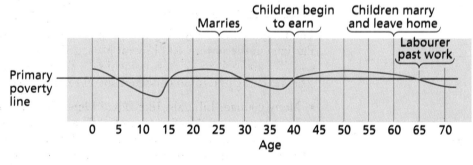

Seebohm Rowntree's poverty line, showing when an individual might be above or below the line.

● **SOURCE 10**

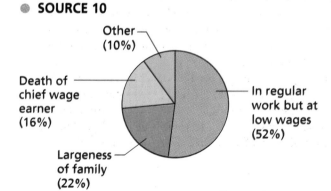

Seebohm Rowntree's analysis of the main reasons for primary poverty, in York, 1900–01.

The two most important things to remember about the work of William and Catherine Booth, Charles Booth and Seebohm Rowntree are:

- They showed that the problem of poverty had not been solved: it was as great as ever.
- They showed that the Victorian idea that poverty was usually the fault of the poor themselves, was simply not true.

Why did poverty become a political issue?

There had always been poor people in Britain. Why did they become an important political issue in the early 1900s?

- Seebohm Rowntree's book, *Poverty: a Study of Town Life*, was read by thousands of people and Charles Booth's books on the labouring poor in London were consulted by hundreds more. Some of these people, like the young MP Winston Churchill, would soon be in a position to do something about the grinding poverty in which millions lived.
- In 1899, the British army began fighting the Boer settlers in South Africa. Young men volunteered to fight and in their thousands they were rejected as unfit. In some industrial areas of Britain, as many as two out of three volunteers were turned down because they failed the army medical examination. This was worrying enough in itself, but there were wider implications. The economies of countries such as Germany and the USA were highly successful because of the skills and hard work of their workforces. It looked as if the British workforce hadn't got the strength or the stamina to compete.
- In 1900, all the socialist groups in Britain came together and formed the Labour Party. This new political party pledged to get better living and working conditions for working people as well as a fairer distribution of the country's wealth. The Liberal Party was afraid that the Labour Party would take members and votes from them.

Enter the Liberal Party

The Liberal Party swept to power in the general election of 1906. In the new Parliament there were 400 Liberal MPs, 157 Conservatives, 83 Irish Nationalists and 29 Labour MPs. Almost immediately the Liberal Government embarked on a far-reaching and unprecedented social reform programme. Why was this?

- Many younger Liberals, like David Lloyd George (Chancellor of the Exchequer) and Winston Churchill (President of the Board of Trade), had been challenging the traditional Liberal view that people should be free to work out their own solutions. These 'New Liberals' believed the State should provide the framework within which everyone could live in security and freedom.
- The 'New Liberals' inside and outside Parliament had read, and were convinced by, the writings of Charles Booth and Seebohm Rowntree. They were impressed by the new understanding that the poor were rarely to blame for their own poverty and were shocked that many people were so poor that they could do nothing to lift themselves out of poverty.
- Towards the end of the nineteenth century, some local authorities had taken on responsibility for such things as providing clean piped water to houses, connecting all houses to sewerage systems, lighting the streets and cleaning them. These schemes, often run by Liberals, showed what could be done on a local scale and raised the possibility of what could be done nationally.

What did the Liberal Government do to help children?

Free school meals (1906)

Local councils were given the power to provide free meals for children from the poorest families. These meals were to be paid for from the local rates. By 1914, over 158,000 children were having free meals once a day, every day.

School medical inspections (1907)

Doctors and nurses went into schools to give pupils compulsory medical checks and recommend any treatment they thought necessary. These checks were free, but until 1912, parents had to pay for any treatment required.

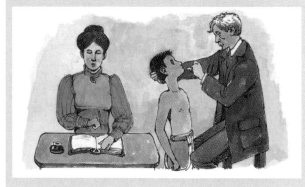

The Children's Act (1908)

This Act, sometimes called the **Children's Charter**, did several things to help children:

- Children became 'protected persons' which meant that their parents could be prosecuted for cruelty against them.
- Poor law authorities were made responsible for visiting and supervising children who had suffered cruelty or neglect.
- All children's homes were to be registered and inspected.
- Children under the age of 14 who had broken the law could no longer be sent to adult prisons.
- Juvenile courts were set up to try children accused of a crime.
- Children who had committed a crime were sent to Borstals that were specially built and equipped to cope with young offenders.
- Children under 14 were not allowed into pubs.
- Shopkeepers could not sell cigarettes to children under 16.

School clinics (1912)

A network of school clinics was set up that provided free medical treatment for children. This was necessary because some parents could not afford the treatment that doctors wanted to give their children as a result of discovering something wrong during their medical inspection.

● **SOURCE 11**

Photograph of a London County Council doctor examining a child in a London school, 1911.

What did the Liberal Government do to help the sick and unemployed?

The Labour Exchanges Act (1909)

A national string of state labour exchanges was set up. This meant that unemployed workers could go to a labour exchange to look for a job instead of having to tramp from workplace to workplace to find work. This was much more efficient both for those looking for work and those offering it.

However, it was the laws Parliament passed to help prevent poverty caused by illness and unemployment that had the greatest impact:

The National Insurance Act (1911)

This set up an insurance scheme that aimed to prevent poverty resulting from illness. Workers could insure themselves against sickness and draw money from the scheme if they fell ill and could not work.

- All manual workers and people in low-paid white-collar jobs had to join.
- Workers paid 4d for insurance stamps which they stuck on a special card.
- Employers contributed 3d for each worker in the scheme.
- The Government contributed 2d for each worker in the scheme.
- If a worker in the scheme fell ill, they got sick pay of 10s a week for 13 weeks and then 5s for a further 13 weeks in any one year.

- Workers in the scheme could get free medical treatment and maternity care.

In the beginning, around ten million men and four million women were covered by national insurance.

The National Insurance Act, Part II (1912)

This part of the National Insurance Act aimed to prevent poverty resulting from unemployment by insuring workers against periods when they were out of work.

- The scheme was open, at the start, to people (mainly men) who worked in trades like shipbuilding and engineering, where there was a great deal of seasonal unemployment.
- Workers, employers and the Government each paid 2d a week for insurance stamps for every worker in the scheme.
- Workers could, when unemployed, be paid 7s 6d a week for up to 15 weeks in any one year.

What did the Liberal Government do to help the elderly?

The Pensions Act (1908)

This gave weekly pensions from government funds to the elderly. The promise to introduce pensions was made in the 1908 budget and became law the following year.

- Everyone over the age of 70 was eligible for a state pension.
- A single person received 5s a week and a married couple 7s 6d (later increased to 10s).

● **SOURCE 12**

A photograph showing elderly men waiting outside the Post Office in Wickhambrook, Suffolk, on the first pension day, 6 January 1909.

How effective were the Liberal Government reforms?

A traditional way of looking at the Liberal Government welfare reforms is to say that they represented a break with the past. No longer did the authorities believe that if people were poor, then it was somehow their own fault. The Liberal Government had made a start on attacking the causes of poverty and were helping the poorest people to lead decent lives. But was this enough?

Did the Liberal reforms help all poor people?

They most certainly did not, and they were not intended to. The two major Liberal reforms, old age pensions and national insurance, were quite limited. Remember that the total population of Britain was around 45 million people.

1 Pensions

Only around half a million elderly people qualified for state old age pensions. This was because the pensions were only for people who:

- were over 70 years old
- had an income of below £21 a year (on a sliding scale up to an income of £31.10 a year after which there was no pension at all)
- were British citizens who had been living in Britain for more than 20 years
- had not been in prison during the ten years before claiming their pension
- had not 'habitually failed to work according to their ability, opportunity and need'.

2 National Insurance

National insurance against sickness initially covered ten million men and four million women. It was only for people who:

- were on low incomes (less than £160 a year)
- made the contributions. It did not cover their dependents.

National insurance against unemployment initially covered around 2.25 million workers, most of them skilled men. It was restricted to:

- trades where seasonal unemployment was common, including building, shipbuilding and engineering.

3 The Poor Law

In 1909, the Liberal Government had a chance to reform the Poor Law when the Royal Commission (set up in 1905) finally reported. The Commission produced two reports. The first recommended reforming the Poor Law, the second abolishing it. The Government did nothing, and the Poor Law remained for another 20 years.

How were the reforms put into action?

The responsibility for carrying out many of the Government's reforms fell on local councils, for example, the central government made it possible for local government to implement reforms such as free school meals. By 1914 over 14 million free school meals per year were being cooked for around 158,000 children. Similarly, although local councils were not forced to set up clinics, by 1914 most were providing some free medical treatment for children.

Opposition to the reforms

These reforms, especially pensions, had to be paid for. To do this, David Lloyd George, as Chancellor of the Exchequer, introduced a budget in 1909 which taxed the rich and the landowners. At first, the House of Lords, which was full of landowners, opposed the budget.

Many people still believed that everyone should look after themselves and their families. They thought it was wrong for the State to step in and help people as this might encourage them to be lazy. It would make them dependent and less able to stand on their own two feet. Sources 13, 14 and 15 explain some of the arguments for and against the reforms.

However, after a general election in January 1910, which the Liberals won, the House of Lords had to agree to the budget.

● SOURCE 13

RICH FARE.
A cartoon from 1909 commenting on Lloyd George's budget.

● SOURCE 14

The provision which is made for the sick and unemployed is grossly inadequate in this country, and yet the working classes have done their best to make provision without the aid of the State. But it is insufficient. The old man has to bear his own burden, while in the case of a young man, who is broken down and who has a wife and family to maintain, the suffering is increased and multiplied. These problems of the sick, of the infirm, of the men who cannot find means of earning a livelihood are problems with which it is the business of the State to deal; they are problems which the State has neglected too long.

Lloyd George speaking in Parliament, June 1908.

● SOURCE 15

The strength of this kingdom, in all its past struggles, has been its great reserve of wealth and the sturdy independent character of its people. The measure which is being pushed through the House of Commons with haste will destroy both. It will extort wealth from its possessors by unjust taxation. It will distribute it in small doles, the most wasteful of all forms of expenditure, and will weaken the character of the people by teaching them to rely, not on their own exertions, but on the State.

A letter to *The Times* newspaper, 3 July 1908.

What have historians said about the Liberal Government reforms?

Historians disagree about the importance of the Liberal reforms of 1906–12. Some see them as the beginnings of the Welfare State; others as a purely economic-based move to improve the health of Britain's workforce.

● SOURCE 16

Two men, David Lloyd George and Winston Churchill, were responsible for launching a great social programme which laid the foundations of a future welfare state.

From C Cross, *The Liberals in Power,* published in 1963.

● SOURCE 17

There were many people who took part in putting together the Liberal reforms who had no idea of creating a 'welfare state' of the type that developed in Britain after 1945. Indeed, many of the Liberals of 1906–14 would have been appalled by that prospect. Key figures, like Lloyd George and Churchill, looked towards the creation of a society in which the worst aspects of poverty would be wiped out. They saw the importance of welfare measures that would act as an alternative to socialism, help the British economy by preventing the physical and mental deterioration of the workers, and provide a measure of social justice which would help attract working class votes without alienating the middle classes.

From J R Hay, *The Origins of the Liberal Welfare State,* published in 1975.

Whatever the interpretation placed upon the Liberal reforms, it is clear that the range of social initiatives undertaken by the Liberals was impressive. The desperately poor were helped and the State took on responsibility for this.

Task

1 You are going to work out how successfully the Liberal Government attacked poverty in the years before the First World War.
   a) Draw up a grid with three headings:

   - Act of Parliament
   - Who did it help?
   - Who was excluded?

   b) Go back through this section and note down, in the first column, the Acts of Parliament that were designed to attack poverty. Then use the information in this section to fill in the other two columns.
   c) Write a paragraph to answer the question 'How successfully did the Liberal Government attack poverty?'

2 Why do you think historians have disagreed about the reasons for the Liberal Government's attack on poverty in the years before the First World War?

Votes for women

Had things changed for the better between 1850 and 1900?

● **SOURCE 1**

In every excellent characteristic, whether mental or physical, the average woman is inferior to the average man. Even in physical beauty the man is superior.

These words were not written by a crank, but by a respected scientist in the middle of the nineteenth century. Most men would have agreed with him.

Victorians believed that a woman's role in life was as a wife and a mother. As a wife, her duty was to obey her husband and do everything she could to make his life as easy as possible. The education that girls received reinforced this view.

Working-class women

Before 1870, most working-class girls did not go to school. A system of state schools was set up in 1870, and in 1880 it was made compulsory for all children between the ages of five and ten to attend. In one way, the results were spectacular. By 1900, 97 per cent of all children could read and write. However, look at Sources 2 and 3.

● **SOURCE 2**

A girl is not necessarily a better woman because she knows the heights of all the mountains in Europe, and can work a fraction in her head; but she is better fitted for the duties she will be called upon to perform if she knows how to wash and tend a child, cook simple food well and thoroughly clean a house.

Written by a school inspector in 1874.

● **SOURCE 3**

Housewifery
Lesson 1: Laying a table. Preparing dinner.
Lesson 2: How to light a fire. Cleaning kitchen flues and grates.
Lesson 4: Bedrooms. Ventilation of room and bed. How to make a bed.

Laundry work
Lesson 1: Preparation for washing day. Rules for drying clothes.
Lesson 7: Removing tea stains, fruit stains, etc. Washing and ironing table linen.
Lesson 9: Washing, starching and ironing collars and cuffs.

Cookery
Lesson 1: Management of stove. Porridge-making.
Lesson 4: Using scraps (remains of joint). Gravy-making. Boiling potatoes. Cocoa-making.

Extracts from a school syllabus for girls in Bristol in 1899.

Task

1 Study Sources 2, 3 and 4. Did the education girls received reinforce their role in society or did it encourage them to look for new roles?

● **SOURCE 4**

A photograph showing girls at school learning to do the laundry in 1908.

Nearly all working-class married women would have to go out to work as they needed the money. One in three had been a domestic servant at some time in her life. Many women worked at home, or in small workshops, sewing or making matchboxes or candles and many others still worked in textile factories.

However, towards the end of the nineteenth century new jobs were appearing. There were jobs in the many new shops that were opening, as well as jobs as typists and on telephone switchboards. Only the luckiest would get one of these jobs and the hours were still long (an 80-hour week in shops). Women often had to leave when they married, and they were paid a great deal less than men doing similar jobs.

● **SOURCE 5**

A photograph showing women working at a telephone switchboard in 1910.

● **SOURCE 6**

A painting showing the crinolines worn by rich women in the nineteenth century. They had so many layers of petticoats that sometimes they could not get through doors. Women tried to achieve a waist of 17 inches!

Middle- and upper-class women

Girls from richer families were usually educated at home by a governess. The main aim of their education was to make them good wives and mothers. They were taught music, singing and drawing – things that would make them an agreeable companion for a future husband. In a sense, they were ornaments for men! This is shown by the clothes they wore – long dresses with tiny waists. They would starve themselves and use corsets to achieve their tiny waists, all because men thought this was feminine. However, towards the end of the nineteenth century things were changing (see Sources 6 and 7).

It was not only in how they dressed that middle-class girls were given more freedom. In the latter half of the nineteenth century, many did attend school, but it was still very difficult for women to go on to higher education or to train for professions like medicine or law. In the 1870s, when Sophia Jex-Blake completed the course to become a doctor, Edinburgh University refused to give her a degree! But things were changing and by 1900, London and Manchester Universities accepted women. Women's colleges had been founded at Oxford and Cambridge, although women still could not be awarded degrees. Several teacher training colleges for women had also opened.

● **SOURCE 7**

This painting shows a dress that gave women more freedom so that they could even take up sport.

New employment opportunities were opening up for middle-class women:

- Teaching (but female teachers had to be single).
- Nursing (the Nightingale School for Nurses was set up in 1860). Nurses had to resign when they married.
- Clerical work. Some middle-class women became typists and telephonists.

By 1900, women could become doctors and architects but were not allowed to be lawyers. Banks and the stock exchange were also closed to women. Men and women still largely did very different types of jobs. When they did the same job, men were paid more (see Source 8).

SOURCE 8

Occupation	Men's wages	Women's wages
Carpet weavers	35s a week	20s a week
Machinists in tailoring	22s 6d a week	11s a week
Civil service typists	£3 a week	£1 a week

A comparison of men's and women's wages around 1900.

Marriage

In the middle of the nineteenth century, women were in a very inferior position within marriage compared to their husbands. When they married, their property passed to their husbands; in fact *they* became the property of their husbands! Husbands could rape and batter their wives and it was virtually impossible for a woman to instigate a divorce.

Women campaigned for changes and by 1900, there were improvements:

- Women could bring divorce cases against their husbands for cruelty, desertion and bigamy.
- Women were allowed to keep their own property after they married.
- A woman no longer had to stay in her husband's home against her will.

However, not everything had changed; wife-battering and marital rape were still legal. Husbands could divorce their wives for adultery, but wives could not divorce their husbands (unless they could prove cruelty as well as adultery). If a divorce did occur, the mother would lose all rights over her children.

Task

1 Between 1850 and 1900 there were many ways in which the position of women improved. List five of these improvements.
2 By 1900 women were still unequal to men in many ways. List five examples of these ways.
3 Do you agree that by 1900 women had largely achieved equality with men?

The arguments for and against votes for women

One of the most important ways in which women did not have equal rights to men was that they were not allowed to vote in parliamentary elections and they were not allowed to become MPs. However, by 1900 'votes for women' had become an important issue and some women (and even a few men) were putting forward strong arguments about why women should have the vote. The arguments were put forward by the two main organisations campaigning for votes for women – the National Union of Women's Suffrage Societies (NUWSS) and the Women's Social and Political Union (WSPU). You will find information about both organisations on pages 34 and 35.

Arguments supporting votes for women

> The vote is a way to get rid of other inequalities.

As we have seen, by 1900 women were still unequal to men in many ways. Some women believed that the only way to change these inequalities was to get the vote. Once women had the vote they could put pressure on Parliament to change other laws. Because Parliament was full of men who had been voted for by men, they passed laws favourable to men. If women had the vote, and if Parliament had some women MPs, laws improving the lives of women were more likely to be passed. Laws could be passed giving women equal pay, giving them equal rights within marriage, and giving them equal rights to divorce. As Source 9 explains, some women also believed it would help get rid of prostitution; if women earned more they would not have to resort to prostitution.

● SOURCE 9

We wish for the vote because there exists a terrible trade of procuring young girls for immoral purposes. Once the girl is seduced it is very difficult for her to return home. She becomes a prostitute. The time has come for women to help and the first step to this lies in winning the vote for without this they have no power. It would be much more difficult for this cruel and wicked traffic to be carried on if it were recognised by the law that women were of the same value and had the same standing as men.

Written by a member of the NUWSS.

● SOURCE 10

It is our duty to make this world a better place for women. If we get the vote, it will mean changed conditions for our less fortunate sisters.

Emmeline Pankhurst.

● SOURCE 11

THE Scylla AND CHARYBDIS OF THE WORKING WOMAN.

A WSPU poster showing the dangers that faced working women.

> The vote will improve men's moral and sexual behaviour.

One of the slogans of the WSPU was 'Votes for Women and Chastity for Men', and some suffragettes like Christabel Pankhurst believed that giving women the vote would help improve men's sexual behaviour. They thought that making women equal to men would make men follow women's much higher moral standards. They saw women as the defenders of virtue, and men as the lustful destroyers of chastity. Christabel Pankhurst thought that pre-marital sex, prostitution and venereal disease would all disappear if women got the vote.

● SOURCE 12

The law of the land, as made and administered by men, protects and encourages the immorality of men, and the sexual exploitation of women.

From *The Great Scourge and How to end it*, a pamphlet written by Christabel Pankhurst in 1913.

● **SOURCE 13**

A photograph of a suffragette selling suffragette leaflets in 1908. 'The Great Scourge' is venereal disease, which was on the increase at this time.

> Women are capable of being involved in politics.

Many people at this time believed in the idea of 'separate spheres'. This said that God had made men and women different, so they should follow different roles in life. Women could have babies and breastfeed them, so they should stay at home in the 'private sphere'. Men were better suited to the 'public sphere' of work and politics.

In the nineteenth century, women had begun challenging this idea. Many had become active in politics in lots of ways. Some women were allowed to vote in local elections, and in 1907 this was extended to all female rate payers. Some, like Christabel Pankhurst, served as Poor Law guardians, while others campaigned to reform workhouses, improve hospitals and change the divorce laws and other inequalities. These women clearly showed that they were capable of understanding and being involved in politics.

> There have been changes in women's roles.

We have seen that through new types of jobs like typing and teaching, many more women were going out to work. Women were also going to university and becoming doctors. In 1888, Annie Besant led women match-makers in a strike for better pay and conditions. In these, and other ways, women were beginning to destroy the idea of 'separate spheres'. If they were active in these public roles, why shouldn't they get the vote as well? Some women saw the vote as the final way in which women had to achieve equality with men.

> Look at what is happening in other countries.

Britain was falling behind other countries. By 1914, many women in the USA had the vote, as well as in New Zealand, parts of Australia, and even the Isle of Man. If in these countries, why not in Britain?

Voting is a 'right' to which women are entitled.

Three times in the nineteenth century the vote was extended to more and more men. After 1884, most men had the vote. There were some attempts to give women the vote but they all failed. This naturally led women to ask when it was going to be their turn, especially since a man's right to vote was based on property qualifications; he was given the vote if he was a householder. Some women owned more property than some men did, they paid more rates and taxes, and yet were not allowed to vote.

As many women argued, why should an illiterate, uneducated male farm labourer have the vote, when the female landowner he worked for, who was educated and literate, did not?

Britain is not a true democracy until women have the vote.

Another argument was that Britain could not claim to be a democratic country if over half of its adult population (the women) did not have the right to vote. Other people banned from voting included criminals and the certified insane. It was absurd to put women in the same category.

● **SOURCE 14**

THE DIGNITY OF THE FRANCHISE.

Qualified Voter: "AH, YOU MAY PAY RATES AN' TAXES, AN' YOU MAY 'AVE RESPONSERBILITIES 'ALL; BUT WHEN IT COMES TO *VOTIN'*, YOU MUST LEAVE IT TO *US MEN!*"

A cartoon published in the early twentieth century.

Task

1 Do you think Source 14 was supporting or criticising votes for women? Use the details in the cartoon to support your answer: look at how the man and the woman have been drawn, and what we are told about them.

● **SOURCE 15**

Women have already equal privileges with men in the matter of voting for district councils, Poor Law guardians, school boards.

The woman householder is called upon to pay the same rates and taxes as if she were a man. Would the authorities take any notice if she were to claim exemption on the ground of sex?

Their labourers on the estate have votes, while the mistress who employs them is not considered competent to have the vote.

From an NUWSS magazine published in 1898.

Arguments against women having the vote

At first, the idea that women should have the vote was seen as so ridiculous that no one attempted to oppose it. However, when the suffragettes began to win support, those opposing them had to take them more seriously. These pages cover the arguments they came up with. Some of them might seem silly to you, but they made sense to a lot of people at the time.

> Women and men have 'separate spheres'.

We have already seen that some people believed that women were suited to the private sphere of life (bringing up children, cooking, looking after the house), while men were more suited to the public sphere of work and politics. Many women did not know anything about the nature of their husband's jobs or their opinions on major political issues. They appeared to be totally absorbed in their domestic lives. This is how the opponents of suffragettes thought it should be. They believed that these separate spheres had been ordained by God and were afraid of the day when the husband came home from work, worn out, only to find his wife at a political meeting and the children and the home neglected. They were convinced that family life would be destroyed if women won the vote.

These ideas had their basis in scientific theories of the time about the physical and psychological differences between men and women. It was believed that women were guided more by their womb than by their brain. They were more prone to hysteria (much of the suffragettes' more extreme actions were put down to this hysteria). They were seen as childish, bad-tempered and fickle because of their reproductive cycle. They lacked logical power and were far too emotional to reach sensible decisions about political issues. Women were intellectually inferior to men because their brains weighed less!

> Most women do not want the vote.

The opponents of the suffragettes argued that the vast majority of women did not want the vote and had no interest in public affairs. They pointed out that only a small fraction of women joined the various suffrage organisations. They were also convinced that the suffragettes were just mad, frustrated spinsters, while normal women were happy to look after their husbands, children and home.

> Women's role is in local affairs.

The anti-suffragettes did believe that women should be active 'citizens', but they thought that this was achieved by contributing to the community, not by voting in national elections. They argued that women's involvement on school boards, as Poor Law guardians, and their work for charities, was all an extension of their domestic role because they were contributing to their local community. Getting involved in national elections was a completely different matter.

> Women are already represented by their husbands.

Some argued that women did not need to have the vote because their husbands would be representing them when they voted. Wives were expected to have the same political views as their husbands; this meant that giving women the vote would be the same as giving husbands two votes!

> It is dangerous to change a system that works.

This point of view was based on the idea that 'if it isn't broken, don't try to fix it'. In other words, the existing political system in Britain worked well. It had, after all, seen Britain become the most powerful country in the world. Making a big change, such as letting women vote, could upset the stability of the system. It was too big a risk to take.

> Women do not fight to defend their country.

This view was based on the idea that people earned the right to vote by being willing to fight for their country. As women could not fight in the army or navy, they did not deserve the vote. There was also the worry that if women got the vote they would not want Britain to fight wars and, as a result, Britain's place in the world would decline.

Task

1 Study the following sources. For each one, explain whether it supports or opposes the idea of women being able to vote.

SOURCE 16

The point of hysterical emotion and unreason is always nearer with women.

Mrs Frederic Harrison, 1909.

SOURCE 17

A poster from around 1910

SOURCE 18

A poster from 1912.

● **SOURCE 19**

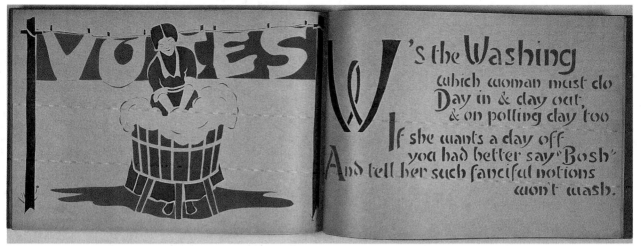

A page from a book published in 1911.

● **SOURCE 20**

They are for the most part hopelessly ignorant of politics, credulous to the last degree, and flickering with gusts of sentiment like a candle in the wind.

Herbert Asquith, 1906.

● **SOURCE 21**

I shall break down all attempts to break down the barrier which nature has placed between men and women. I believe I am supported by the vast majority of women in this country.

Henry Labouchere MP, around 1905.

● **SOURCE 22**

A poster from 1910

The suffragists and the suffragettes

Everyone campaigning for the vote for women agreed on what they wanted, but they did not agree about the best way to achieve it. Some used peaceful methods; they were called suffragists, and their organisation was called the National Union of Women's Suffrage Societies (NUWSS). Others were prepared to use violence; they were called suffragettes, and their organisation was called the Women's Social and Political Union (WSPU).

The suffragists

The campaign for the vote started in the nineteenth century. In 1866, campaigners collected 1500 signatures for a petition demanding the vote for women. In 1867, Lydia Becker formed the Manchester Society for Women's Suffrage. Similar societies were set up in London, Bristol, Birmingham and Edinburgh. After the setback of the rejection of the petition of 1866, these women kept the cause alive by writing, lecturing and organising more petitions.

The turning point came in 1897 when Millicent Fawcett linked many of the different women's organisations into the National Union of Women's Suffrage Societies. She became its president for over 20 years. There was now a national organisation, and this made the women's movement far more powerful. By 1914, it had more than 400 branches all over the country and over 100,000 members (see Source 24). It was a democratic organisation with members electing a president and committee which made decisions.

● **SOURCE 23**

A photograph of Millicent Fawcett.

● **SOURCE 24**

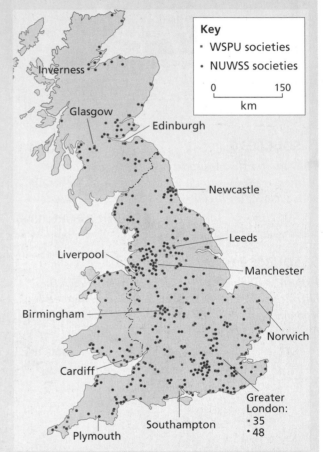

Map showing branches of the NUWSS and the WSPU.

Many of the women members were middle class and were often involved in other women's rights issues, for example improving the rights of married women. However, the NUWSS did have working-class members as well, especially in the north of England, in cotton towns like Bolton and Blackburn. Men were also allowed to join, and some did!

The suffragettes

The WSPU was founded by Emmeline Pankhurst and her two daughters Christabel and Sylvia in 1903. Source 25, from Emmeline Pankhurst's autobiography, tells us the aims of the suffragettes.

SOURCE 25

To secure for women the Parliamentary vote as it is or may be granted to men. To limit our membership to women and to be satisfied with nothing but action on our question. Deeds, not Words, was to be our motto.

Our members are absolutely single-minded; they concentrate all their forces on one object, political equality with men. No member of the WSPU divides her attention between suffrage and other social reforms.

From Emmeline Pankhurst, *My Own Story*, 1914.

SOURCE 26

A photograph of Emmeline Pankhurst with Christabel and Sylvia.

The WSPU had branches all over the country (see Source 24), but its leaders were not chosen by the members. It was very much controlled by the Pankhursts.

The Pankhursts formed the WSPU because they were impatient with the peaceful methods of the suffragists. In 1905, Christabel Pankhurst and Annie Kenney demonstrated the new methods of the suffragettes by attending a meeting of the Liberal Party. They began shouting out 'Will the Liberal Government give women the vote?' The police tried to remove them and Christabel spat in a policeman's face and then hit him in the mouth. She was arrested and charged with assault. When found guilty she was given the choice between a fine and seven days' imprisonment. She went to prison. The case attracted massive publicity and when Christabel was released a crowd of 2000 people was waiting to welcome her. The suffragettes learned a simple lesson from this episode: militancy was news.

Men were not allowed to join the WSPU and Christabel, in particular, was very anti-men. In 1906, the WSPU moved its headquarters from Manchester to London. After that date it recruited mainly middle- and upper-class women and the membership of working-class women fell.

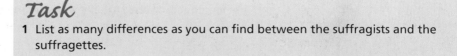

Task

1 List as many differences as you can find between the suffragists and the suffragettes.

The main events 1906–14

In 1906, the Liberal Party won a landslide victory in the general election. The hopes of women campaigners were raised because it was known that many Liberal MPs supported the idea of votes for women. However, the leaders of the party were not so keen and the battle was going to be long and hard.

Date	Main events
1906	Liberal landslide victory. The Prime Minister, Sir Henry Campbell-Bannerman, supports votes for women but ministers are divided.
Oct 1906	NUWSS continues campaign of petitions and meetings. WSPU members protest in the House of Commons. They are arrested and sent to prison. WSPU starts campaign of noisily opposing MPs at by-elections.
Feb 1907	The NUWSS organises procession in London. Over 3000 women march. Called the 'Mud March' because of the bad weather.
1908	Herbert Asquith becomes Prime Minister. He is against votes for women but tells the women to prove there is popular support for the idea.
June 1908	Both the suffragists and the suffragettes organise massive processions in London with supporters coming from all over the country. However, Asquith does nothing and in frustration suffragettes start smashing windows in Downing Street and later chain themselves to railings. Both NUWSS and WSPU growing in members.
Late 1908	Split between NUWSS and WSPU starts. The suffragists are worried that the suffragettes' activities are making the Government hostile to votes for women.
1909	More WSPU members sent to prison. Demand to be treated as political prisoners and go on hunger strike. Government does not want dead women on its hands and starts force-feeding them.
1910	The WSPU calls off its violent protests when Asquith agrees to work with them and the NUWSS to produce a Conciliation Bill giving women the vote. At first it does well in the House of Commons but then Asquith begins to stall. The WSPU protests and this turns into 'Black Friday', a fight with the police resulting in many women being physically and sexually assaulted by officers.

1911	The WSPU again call a truce in the hope that the Conciliation Bill will be passed. The Government stalls again, then announces it is dropping the Bill. It introduces a new Reform Bill to give more votes to men. The WSPU is furious and re-starts its campaign of violence.
1912	The WSPU begins a massive campaign of window-smashing. Many arrests follow. The WSPU headquarters are raided and some of its leaders arrested. Christabel Pankhurst flees to Paris. Mass hunger strikes in prisons across the country for political status. The authorities respond with force-feeding.
1913	Violence increases, for example, buildings bombed and burnt down, letters in letter boxes destroyed, turf at race courses burned. The Government introduces the 'Cat and Mouse Act' – women were allowed to go on hunger strike in prison. They were released when they became ill, only to be rearrested when they recovered.
June 1913	Emily Davison kills herself by running out in front of the King's horse at the Derby. Meanwhile, the NUWSS is desperately trying to win over public opinion. In the Women's Pilgrimage, women walk to London from all over Britain, raising thousands of pounds on the way.
1914	WSPU violence escalates. Public opinion now firmly against the suffragettes. Women banned from art galleries and museums. The First World War begins and both the suffragettes and the suffragists stop all their activities and help the war effort. The Government releases all WSPU prisoners.

Task

1 Draw a timeline 1906–14 and write on it the ten most important events.
2 Copy and complete the following graph by drawing a line showing how votes for women became more or less likely throughout this period.

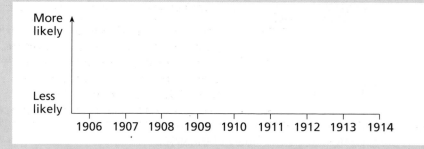

Different ways of winning the vote

As you have realised by now, many different strategies were used to try to win the vote for women. These can be divided into peaceful and violent methods.

It is important that you develop a view about which type of methods did the cause most good, and which did it most harm. This issue is discussed later.

Peaceful methods

Propaganda

Both the suffragists and the suffragettes made effective use of propaganda. The WSPU published a newspaper called *Votes for Women* which argued the case and gave the suffragettes great publicity. By 1914, it had a circulation of 40,000. The suffragettes were very good propagandists. Their slogan 'Votes for Women' was found everywhere, while they used their colours of purple, white and green to sell clothes, dolls, jewellery, belts and many other items. Shops wanted to sell goods to women and new fashions were produced featuring the suffragette colours. Even the wrapper on one type of bread was printed with 'Votes for Women' on it.

Particularly effective were the WSPU's propaganda posters, postcards and leaflets. Sources 27–29 are examples of propaganda items.

● **SOURCE 28**

A suffragette poster commenting on the 'Cat and Mouse Act' of 1913.

● **SOURCE 27**

A selection of badges and brooches in the purple, white and green colours of the WSPU.

● **SOURCE 29**

The wardresses forced me on to a bed and the two doctors came in with them, and while I was held down a tube was inserted. It is two yards long with a funnel at the end – there is a glass junction in the middle to see if the liquid is passing. The end is put up one nostril, one day, and the other nostril, the other. Great pain is experienced during the process, the drums of the ear seem to be bursting, a horrible pain in the throat and the breast. The tube is pushed down 20 inches.

The doctor holding the funnel end pours the liquid down; about a pint of milk, sometimes egg and milk are used. Before and after use, they test my heart. The after-effects are a feeling of faintness, a sense of pain in the diaphragm or breast bone, and in the nose and ears. I was very sick on the first occasion after the tube was withdrawn.

From a leaflet published in 1909 entitled *Fed by Force, a Statement by Mrs Mary Leigh, who is still in Birmingham Gaol.*

Meetings and demonstrations

Both the NUWSS and the WSPU held many public meetings. Some of these were huge and were held in buildings like the Royal Albert Hall in London. Other meetings were held in the open air in places like Trafalgar Square and on village greens all over Britain. Many people at the time thought it was unladylike for women to be involved in these kinds of events. Despite this, the demonstrations grew larger and larger with numbers over 20,000 not unusual. The NUWSS Women's Pilgrimage in 1913 was a great success, with thousands of women taking part and the newspapers reporting the event very favourably because of the peaceful way in which it was carried out. The demonstrations were great spectacles with banners, flags and sometimes women dressing up as figures like Joan of Arc. They certainly kept the issue of votes for women in the public eye and on the front pages of the newspapers.

● **SOURCE 30**

A photograph of suffragettes demonstrating on a boat on the River Thames, opposite the House of Commons in 1908.

● **SOURCE 31**

A photograph of a suffragette procession in June 1911.

Putting pressure on Parliament

Ultimately it was Parliament that the campaigners had to win over so much of their effort was directed at MPs. Petitions were drawn up and sent to Parliament. The petition in 1910 in support of the Conciliation Bill contained over 250,000 signatures! Women met with MPs to try to persuade them to support votes for women. MPs who did support the cause were helped in election campaigns by women who canvassed for them.

Civil disobedience

Another argument was that, as you could only vote if you paid taxes, those who couldn't vote shouldn't have to pay taxes, so many women refused to pay. Some also boycotted the 1911 census, saying that if they couldn't vote they wouldn't be part of the official record of the day.

Violent or illegal methods

Attacking property

Window-smashing was one of the first types of violence used by the suffragettes. It started as a spontaneous reaction to the repeated failure of suffrage bills in Parliament, but later the WSPU leadership used it as a deliberate tactic. Emmeline Pankhurst said 'the argument of the broken window pane is the most valuable argument in modern politics'. The windows of government offices were the favourite targets, but the buildings of newspapers, gentlemen's clubs and shops also suffered.

Arson started in a big way in 1913 when Emily Davison planted a bomb at Lloyd George's newly-built house in Surrey. It was badly damaged. This was a strange action to take since Lloyd George was a leading supporter of giving women the vote!

The post was a target as well as buildings. Suffragettes would pour chemicals into letter boxes, destroying all the letters inside.

Other attacks on property included:

- attacks on works of art in art galleries (the suffragette who tried to destroy a valuable painting in the National Portrait Gallery was called 'Slasher Mary' by the newspapers)
- the cutting of telegraph wires
- the burning of messages like 'No Votes, No Golf' into golf courses by acid.

● **SOURCE 32**

A photograph of five suffragettes holding a broken window in its frame, 1912.

● **SOURCE 33**

A photograph of a house attacked by suffragette arsonists In 1913. The house belonged to a Liberal MP.

● **SOURCE 34**

April 2. — Church fired at Hampstead Garden Suburb.
April 3. — Four houses fired at Hampstead Garden Suburb.
April 4. — Mansion near Chorley Wood destroyed by fire; bomb explosion at Oxted station; empty train wrecked by bomb explosion at Devonport; famous pictures damaged at Manchester.
April 5. — Ayr racecourse stand burnt: £3,000 damage; attempt to destroy Kelso racecourse grandstand.

April 6. — House fired at Potter's Bar; mansion destroyed at Norwich.
April 8. — Plot to destroy Crystal Palace stands before the Football Cup tie.
April 11. — Council schools, Gateshead, set on fire.
April 13. — Mansion fired at St. Leonard's: damage £9,000; Home Office order prohibits Suffragette meetings.
April 19. — Attempt to wreck Smeaton's famous Eddystone Lighthouse on Plymouth Hoe.

April 20. — Attempt to blow up offices of 'York Herald', York, with a bomb.
April 23. — Attempt to burn Minster Church, Isle of Thanet.
April 24. — Bomb exploded at County Council offices, Newcastle.
April 26. — Railway carriage destroyed by fire at Teddington.
April 30. — Boathouse burned at Hampton Court: £3,500 damage; Suffragettes' headquarters seized by police, five leaders arrested.

An extract from *The Suffragette*, December 1913. It lists examples of suffragette attacks on property in the month of April.

Attacking people

Sometimes individuals were singled out by the suffragettes for attack, for example doctors who refused to denounce force-feeding. One prison doctor who worked at Holloway Prison was attacked on his way to work with a rhino whip. You have already read about Christabel Pankhurst spitting at, and hitting, a police officer. On another occasion, an axe was thrown at the Prime Minister and only narrowly missed him.

Another form of attack was to heckle politicians and disrupt their meetings. The suffragettes were often thrown out of meetings and many were sent to prison. But every time this happened, the movement gained more publicity. When the Liberal Party banned women from their meetings, suffragettes hid under platforms and on one occasion even swung down into a meeting on ropes, through the skylights.

Hunger strikes

Hunger strikes started in 1909 as a way of forcing the authorities to recognise suffragette prisoners as political prisoners rather than just ordinary criminals. The attraction of hunger strikes for the WSPU was that they won sympathy for the prisoners. *Votes for Women* was full of stories about the agonies these women suffered. These accounts grew more harrowing when the authorities decided to start force-feeding the women who were refusing to eat. Posters like the one in Source 28 on page 38 were sent all over the country. Some women barricaded themselves into their cells and hosepipes of cold water were used to end their protests. The hunger strikes put the Government on the back foot for a while, until they retaliated with the 'Cat and Mouse Act' (see page 44).

Which methods worked best?

There were three reasons why the suffragettes turned to violent methods:

- They thought that peaceful methods were not having any success.
- The Government banned them from meetings and so peaceful protest was denied them.
- The Government started to use violence against them.

Were the new methods effective? Many historians have argued that violence was a mistake because it turned the public and the Liberal Government against the idea of votes for women. It also allowed opponents to argue that the violence showed that women were not responsible enough to have the vote. The suffragettes argued that most reforms in history had only been achieved through violence. They added that women had been working for the vote peacefully for many years and had been completely ignored. Their methods had put the issue on the front pages of the newspapers.

● **SOURCE 35**

A photograph of a suffragette struggling with a policeman on what was known as Black Friday, November 1910 (see page 43).

SOURCE 36

A photograph of Emmeline and Christabel Pankhurst in prison.

The reaction of the authorities

The Liberal Government did not have a clear position on the issue of votes for women. The Prime Minister, Asquith, was definitely against the idea. Most Liberal MPs were probably in favour but did not feel strongly about it. Time and time again, the Government promised to do something and then found an excuse not to.

The Government dealt with protesters harshly, even before they used violence. This suggests that the Government was hostile to the women from the beginning and that its harsh actions were not merely a reaction to the later violent methods of the suffragettes.

First, women were banned from Liberal meetings, but much worse was to come on Black Friday in November 1910. When the women protesters tried to enter Parliament to support the Conciliation Bill (see page 36), the police reacted brutally. Source 37 contains some of the women's accounts of what happened.

SOURCE 37

- *Several times constables and plain-clothes men who were in the crowd passed their arms round me from the back and clutched hold of my breasts.*
- *One policeman put his arm around me and seized my left breast, nipping it and wringing it very painfully, saying as he did so, 'You have been wanting this for a long time haven't you?'*
- *The police deliberately tore my under-garments, using the most foul language. They seized me by the hair and forced me up the steps on my knees. I was then flung into the crowd outside.*

Eye-witness accounts from women involved in the protest.

Force-feeding

Once the protesters were in prison, the authorities tried to humiliate them. They were treated as ordinary criminals; they were not allowed to speak and were called by their number rather than by their name. They had to scrub the cell floors, empty their slops (chamber pots), clean their tin bowls, and they could only have a bath once a week. Going on hunger strike was a reaction to these conditions. The authorities responded by force-feeding prisoners. This was a terrifying experience as Source 38 makes clear. Do you think the Government treated suffragettes in this way because they were hostile to them or because they were concerned about the health of the women on hunger strike?

SOURCE 38

People were held down by force, flung on the floor, tied to chairs and iron bedsteads while the tube was forced up the nostrils. After each feeding the nasal pain gets worse. The wardress endeavoured to make one prisoner open her mouth by sawing the edge of a cup along her gums. The broken edge caused laceration and severe pain. Food into the lung of one unresisting prisoner immediately caused severe choking, vomiting and persistent coughing. She was hurriedly released next day suffering from pneumonia and pleurisy. We cannot believe that any of our colleagues will agree that this form of prison treatment is justly described in Mr McKenna's words as necessary medical treatment.

From the medical journal *The Lancet*, August 1912.

The Cat and Mouse Act

The next reaction by the Government was the Prisoners, Temporary Discharge for Health, Act, popularly known as the 'Cat and Mouse Act', of 1913. This allowed hunger strikers to be released to recover their health. Once they were recovered they could be re-arrested and sent back to prison to serve the rest of their sentence. When it was discussed in Parliament, a few MPs did speak against it. They criticised it because it punished the women several times over. Despite these protests it was passed by 296 votes to 43. The following account by Christabel Pankhurst shows how the Act worked and how suffragettes responded. In 1913, Emmeline Pankhurst was in and out of prison 12 times. As a result, she grew weaker and weaker.

● **SOURCE 39**

The licence was read to Mother and she took it and tore it into shreds, saying 'I have no intention of observing these conditions. You release me knowing perfectly well that I shall never voluntarily return to this place.'

The Government kept a police watch to prevent Mother's escape. Two detectives and a constable were posted outside the door of the nursing home to which she went. Two taxi-cabs were kept in readiness for pursuit. Several days later Mother announced that, weak as she was, she would speak at a great WSPU meeting that had been arranged. As she left the house she was arrested. Five days she was kept, fasting, in prison, and then released for seven days.

Christabel Pankhurst writing in her memoirs, *Unshackled: The Story of How We Won the Vote*, published in 1959.

The reaction of the Press

Some newspapers like *The Times* were totally against the idea of women having the vote. As Source 41 shows, it reported events in a biased way. The women were often called lunatics, and their behaviour was explained as a result of hysteria. However, it would be a mistake to say that the newspapers were generally against female suffrage. Indeed most probably supported it, but also felt that they had to condemn the violent methods used by the suffragettes. Whenever the campaigners used peaceful methods there was much support for them in the newspapers, and when the demonstrators were assaulted sexually, as on Black Friday, papers like the *Daily Mirror* carried lots of photographs.

● **SOURCE 40**

With sure and certain steps the cause of women's suffrage is marching to victory. Saturday's remarkable procession in London served as a prelude to the inevitable triumph. This beautiful pageant was one of the most impressive demonstrations that London has ever witnessed.

The *Daily Chronicle*, 1911.

● **SOURCE 41**

The suffragettes are regrettable by-products of our civilisation, out with their hammers and their bags full of stones because of dreary, empty lives and high-strung, over-excitable natures.

The *Times*, 1912.

The reaction of the public

Despite all their efforts, or perhaps because of them, the suffragettes did not seem to succeed in winning over the majority of the men in the country. The sources that follow show how most men felt about them, although it must not be forgotten that some men did support and join the NUWSS.

● **SOURCE 42**

Three young men meeting a woman who was carrying a can of tar and suffragist literature, approached and asked her if she was a suffragist. This being admitted, the men, it is reported, tore off nearly all her clothing, saturated it with tar and set fire to it.

News of the World, April 1913.

● **SOURCE 43**

On Saturday night two women distributing suffragist literature at Lyon's Corner House, were pelted with cutlery, sugar, bread and cake. The Suffragettes were eventually placed in a lift. In the hall however hundreds of diners were reinforced by people from outside. For about a quarter of an hour the women were imprisoned in the lift with missiles being thrown at them through the cage.

The Times, 1914.

● **SOURCE 44**

Put me upon an island where the girls are few

Put me among the most ferocious lions in the zoo

Put me in a prison and I'll never fret

But for pity's sake don't put me near a suffering-gette.

A popular song of the time.

Did the violent methods of the suffragettes help?

Yes

- They made female suffrage front page news. They brought it to the attention of the public and the Government.
- Once the issue of votes for women had been raised, and once it had received so much publicity, it was not going to go away. Sooner or later, women would be given the vote.
- There is evidence that, as time passed, the idea of women having the vote was no longer so strange. People were gradually getting used to the idea and beginning to accept it.
- Asquith was already firmly against women getting the vote, so the violent methods did not make things any worse. Asquith's views, and his Government's harsh treatment of the suffragettes, were not caused by the violence of the suffragettes.

- The violence played into the hands of the Government. It gave them an excuse not to give in to the suffragettes. They could argue that it was wrong to give in to violence.
- There were times when the Government appeared to be close to agreeing to female suffrage, but it could not be seen to be giving in to violence.
- The violence turned moderate men, especially moderate MPs, against the idea of votes for women. This is why bills in the House of Commons to give women the vote were always defeated.
- The violence supported the view that women were not responsible enough to have the vote. They were too emotional and hysterical.
- In 1913 and 1914, the NUWSS was growing in popularity at the expense of the WSPU. Some women were turning away from violence.

No

● **SOURCE 45**

They are for the most part hopelessly ignorant of politics, credulous to the last degree, and flickering with gusts of sentiment like a candle in the wind.

Asquith's views on women in 1906.

● **SOURCE 46**

In my opinion, far from having injured the movement they have done more during the last twelve months to bring it within the region of practical politics than we have been able to accomplish in the same number of years.

Millicent Fawcett speaking in 1906 about the suffragettes.

● **SOURCE 47**

I think they would rather lose women's suffrage than give up their own way of demonstrating.

Millicent Fawcett speaking about the suffragettes in 1913.

● **SOURCE 48**

We are not destroying Orchid Houses, breaking windows, cutting telegraph wires, injuring golf courses, in order to win the approval of the people who were attacked. If the general public were pleased with what we are doing, that would be a proof that our warfare is ineffective. We don't intend that you should be pleased.

Emmeline Pankhurst in February 1913.

● **SOURCE 49**

Haven't the suffragettes the sense to see that the very worst way of campaigning for the vote is to try to intimidate or blackmail a man into giving them what he would gladly give otherwise?

Lloyd George in 1913.

Task

1 Write three or four sentences about each of Sources 45–49, explaining whether they show that the suffragettes did more harm than good.

Winning the vote

How close were women to winning the vote in 1914? Here are two different views, one from Christabel Pankhurst and one from an historian.

● **SOURCE 50**

Suffragette activity was at its greatest height. In the prisons, in the courts, heroic women were fighting; militants roved the country challenging the Government. Public meetings were held on a large scale.

The Government still braved it out; but a fatal day of political reckoning was awaiting them, if they delayed justice too long, at the general election. After nearly nine years of unceasing and increasing militancy the women were winning. The Government was getting afraid of the loss of votes.

Christabel Pankhurst in her memoirs, *Unshackled*, published in 1959.

● **SOURCE 51**

By the end of July 1914 the WSPU had become a rump of the large and superbly organised movement it had once been. The tactics employed by the WSPU had failed to force the Liberals to grant women the vote because they lacked broad appeal. A number of politicians who earlier had been sympathetic had been alienated and extreme militancy had also alienated substantial sections of the general public.

From Andrew Rosen, *Rise Up, Women!*, published in 1974.

Suddenly, in August 1914, the situation completely changed. Britain was at war with Germany. Emmeline and Christabel Pankhurst had no hesitation in stopping the suffrage campaign and encouraging members to support the war effort. The NUWSS followed suit, although not with the same enthusiasm.

By 1918, one million more women were at work than had been in 1914. Many historians argue that in 1918 women were given the vote as a reward for their war work: women had shown they could act responsibly, in marked contrast to their earlier irresponsible behaviour, that had achieved nothing but a postponement of the granting of the vote.

We should not automatically accept this view. There are other historians who argue that the activities of the WSPU and the NUWSS were getting very close to winning the vote by 1914. Some even claim that the war held up the winning of the vote. The next section should help you decide what your view is.

Different reactions to the war

You can read about the work women did in the First World War in Unit 3. It is important to remember that both the WSPU and the NUWSS helped the Government in recruiting and organising women workers.

The WSPU

Given their earlier enmity, the suffragettes and the Government worked together amazingly well to encourage women to go out to work. With so many men leaving to fight in Europe, Britain was short of millions of workers by 1915. Unless workers could be found for the factories and farms, Britain's role in the war might have ground to a halt. The WSPU's funds and organisation were used to help the Government. In 1915, the WSPU organised the 'Women's Right to Serve' march (see Sources 52 and 53). The suffragette leaders became more patriotic than many men. They renamed their paper *Britannia* and their organisation became the Women's Party instead of the WSPU. They demanded that military conscription be introduced and went round giving white feathers (symbols of cowardice) to any men not in military uniform. However, not all the suffragettes agreed with this approach. Sylvia Pankhurst, a pacifist, formed a breakaway organisation which concentrated on social work and on criticising the war.

● SOURCE 52

It was impossible for the spectators not to feel touched and stirred and proud of these women of England as they trooped through the rain with one fixed aim – the serving of their country in the hour of its need. At points all along the route were little tables – the women's recruiting stations – at which women were signing on. Here and there groups of soldiers cheered the women, as well they might. The heart of every man went out to them, they were the true women of England, the women of whom to be proud.

From the *Daily Express*, 19 July 1915.
This extract was reprinted in *The Suffragette* on 23 July 1915.

● SOURCE 53

A photograph of landgirls on the Women's Right to Serve march in July 1915.

The NUWSS

Millicent Fawcett supported the war effort, declaring in August 1914, 'Women, your country needs you.' However, she opposed conscription and the giving of white feathers. The NUWSS set up an employment register in 1915 and recruited many women to replace the men who had gone to the Front. It even ran training schools to train women for the new work they were to do, for example one in Notting Hill trained women to be welders. It also organised hospital units on the front lines of the war. These units employed all-female teams of doctors, nurses and ambulance drivers.

However, the NUWSS never forgot the real reason for its existence: winning the vote. Meetings were still held and petitions were still signed; this ensured that pressure was kept on Parliament. Some women even left the NUWSS so that they could devote all their time to campaigning for the vote.

Task

1 How different were the reactions of the WSPU and the NUWSS to the coming of war?

How the vote was won

After all the struggles for the vote before the war, the way women eventually won the vote was almost an anti-climax. Preparations for reform started in 1916. This was mainly because thousands of men who had volunteered to fight for their country had lost their right to vote; the law said that anyone away from home for more than a year lost this right. The Government obviously had to do something about this and started to plan. Millicent Fawcett and the NUWSS heard about this and began to put pressure on the Government to consider also the issue of votes for women. A Conference on Electoral Reform was set up to produce recommendations. In 1917, it recommended that some women should be given the vote. Later in 1917, when the House of Commons voted on the issue, 385 MPs voted in favour, and 55 voted against.

On 6 February 1918, the Bill was given royal assent and became law. This is what it did:

- Women over the age of 30 were given the vote.
- Women over the age of 30 were allowed to become MPs.
- All men over the age of 21 were given the vote.

This meant that out of an electorate of 21 million, 8 million were women. This was not everything that women had fought for as they still did not have the vote on the same terms as men. There were two reasons for this:

- The Government was worried about there being more women voters than men.
- The Government was worried about young women being 'flighty' and not responsible enough to have the vote.

● **SOURCE 54**

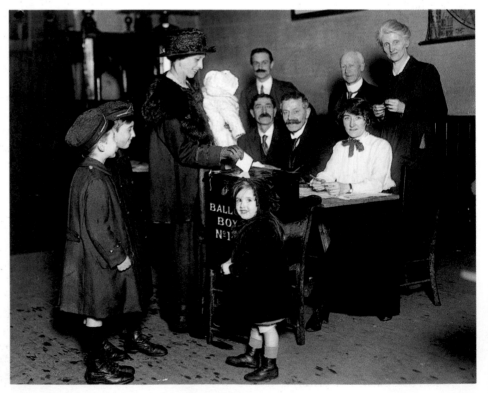

A photograph of a mother, with her four children, voting in the general election in December 1918.

Why did women get the vote in 1918?

You now know a lot about the events that led to women getting the vote. It's now time to review them.

There are two issues to consider in answering the question of why women got the vote in 1918:

- Why was the idea of women getting the vote being considered at all?
- Why did they get the vote in 1918 in particular?

Why was the idea of women getting the vote being considered at all?

Many historians argue that both the NUWSS and WSPU made votes for women an issue that would not go away. They claim that without the activities of the suffragists and the suffragettes the idea of giving women the vote might not have been considered in 1918. Others argue that the violent tactics of the suffragettes did their cause no good at all and made Prime Minister Asquith, and his Government, determined not to give in to violence. However, the idea of votes for women had been put on the front pages of the newspapers. It was constantly talked about. It was going to happen sooner or later. It is probably fair to conclude that all the campaigning created a situation in which giving women the vote became very possible. However, exactly when and how had not yet been decided.

Why was 1918 the year they got the vote?

The answer to this simple question is very complicated. Some of the contributing factors are outlined below. Note how many of them are to do with the work women did in the war.

- Lloyd George replaced Asquith as Prime Minister in 1916. He was more sympathetic to the idea of votes for women.
- The need for reform in any case because of soldiers who had lost the right to vote by being abroad for a long time. This became an opportunity to include women's rights.
- The war gave MPs a convenient excuse to give up their opposition to votes for women. The war work of women had destroyed many of their arguments. They could now change their minds without looking stupid.
- Many men were genuinely impressed by women's contribution to the war effort. They had shown that they were mature and sensible, and were capable of doing most jobs. The country owed them a lot – without them Britain might have lost the war.

- One of the arguments against giving women the vote had been that they could not take part in the defence of their country. This argument had obviously been destroyed.
- Conservative MPs were happy that women under 30 would not get the vote. They had been worried that young working-class women, like the munitions workers, would vote Labour.
- Liberal and Labour MPs were happy that all women over 30 were getting the vote. This meant that working-class women, as well as middle and upper class, could vote, so they would not all vote Conservative.
- The Government was afraid that the suffragettes would restart their campaigning after the war. How would it look if they started to lock up the very women who had helped win the war?

However, granting the vote to women in 1918 was not a foregone conclusion.

- Many men, especially those in trade unions, did not welcome women workers in the First World War. They were worried that they would work for lower wages and take their jobs. They were not impressed by the work women did!
- Some women did not support the war effort, for example, Sylvia Pankhurst. She campaigned against the war. Some members of the NUWSS continued to campaign for votes for women. Did the Government really feel it wanted to reward these women?
- The women who did much of the really dangerous, hard, and crucial work in the war were young and working class, for example, the munitions workers. And yet they were not given the vote in 1918!

Task

1 Sort out the points above into three groups. Points that suggest:
   a) The vote was won because of war work.
   b) The vote was won because of the campaigns before the war.
   c) The vote was won because of other reasons.
2 Read Sources 55 and 56 on page 52, which are the explanations given by two MPs who changed their minds about votes for women. What different arguments do Asquith and Bonar Law put forward for changing their minds?

● **SOURCE 55**

What are you to do with women? I have no special desire to bring women within the franchise, but I have received a great many representations from those who speak for them, and I am bound to say they present an unanswerable case. If we are to bring in a new class of electors on grounds of State service [a reference to the returning soldiers], they point out that during this War the women of this country have rendered as effective service in the conduct of the war as any other class of the community – they fill our munitions factories, they are doing work which men had to perform before.

Asquith speaking in August 1916 when the question of reform of voting rights was being debated.

● **SOURCE 56**

Since the War began women have refrained from the kind of agitation which alienated people from their cause. They have said, 'So long as there is no extension of the franchise to men we will say nothing, but the moment there is an extension of this kind we will fight for ours.' There really is the problem, as I see it, in a nutshell. You cannot avoid this controversy.

Andrew Bonar Law speaking in 1916. He was Chancellor of the Exchequer in Lloyd George's wartime government.

Task

1 You are now ready to answer this essay question:

'Was the work women did in the war the most important reason why they were given the vote in 1918?'

A writing frame has been provided to help you organise your thoughts and get started. Copy out each section below. The notes in brackets give you some help with finishing each section. You should be able to write the perfect essay!

There were many reasons why women got the vote in 1918. The work of the suffragists and suffragettes was very important.

(Explain the contribution made by the suffragists. Then explain the contribution made by the suffragettes. Discuss how far the violence of the suffragettes helped or hindered the cause.)

The work done by women during the war was also an important factor.

(Explain the arguments for saying that women's work in the war was important.)

Some historians claim that the war was not that important.

(Explain how it can be argued that the war held up the granting of the vote; explain how other factors like the need to give returning soldiers the vote were important; also explain that many of the women who worked in the war were not given the vote.)

In conclusion, I think the most important reason for women getting the vote in 1918 was . . .
The reasons for this are . . .

Britain during the First World War

3

On Monday 4 August 1914, Great Britain declared war on Germany. It was a Bank Holiday Monday, and people were enjoying the sunshine on beaches and in the countryside, in city parks and village pubs. Few could have guessed at the horrors that lay ahead. Most of those who knew, or cared, that war had been declared, thought it would be a 'great lark' and would be 'over by Christmas'. But this war was to be unlike any other. Previous wars had been fought, largely, far away and by small professional armies. This war was to involve millions of fighting men and touch every family in every home in the country. For the first time, Britain was facing total war.

How were civilians affected by the war?

Recruitment: How were enough men found to fight?

Volunteers

When war broke out, Britain had a small army of around 250,000 professional soldiers. Lord Kitchener, the Secretary of State for War, informed the Government that he would need a fighting force of at least one million men. Clearly, something had to be done, and done quickly. The Government began a massive recruitment drive. It set up recruitment offices in every town and city; it commissioned posters and pamphlets urging young men to join up; politicians toured the country making stirring, patriotic speeches. The campaign was hugely successful. Indeed, it was so successful that barracks were overflowing and there were not enough rifles to go round. There was a frenzy of enthusiasm; complete orchestras, football teams and bus depots joined up together and the army kept them together in 'Pals' Battalions'. No one, it seemed, wanted to be left out. A total of 500,000 men signed up in the first month and, by March 1916, over 2.5 million men had volunteered to join 'Kitchener's Army'.

● SOURCE 1

This is one of the earliest, and most famous, recruiting posters. Published in 1914, it shows Lord Kitchener pointing an accusing finger, or so it seemed, at every young man in the country.

The army, of course, benefited from this recruiting campaign. But there was a downside. Families were deprived of husbands, fathers and sons. Whole villages and towns, offices and workshops, lost almost all their young men on the same day. And what of the young men themselves? Many would never return; of those who did, many would be so mentally or physically scarred that they would never again be able to live life to the full in their families and communities.

● **SOURCE 2**

In September 1914, Lord Derby, who owned large parts of the county of Lancashire, held a recruitment meeting in the Lancashire glass-blowing town of St Helens. He wanted to raise a local battalion. About 1000 men volunteered immediately. They were mainly working-class men: glass makers and coal miners, clerks and shop assistants. This photograph shows the St Helens Pals' Battalion, marching to war. Nearly half of them did not return.

Conscription

It slowly became clear that the war was not going to be over by Christmas. It was going to last considerably longer. Casualties increased, dead and wounded soldiers had to be replaced, and it became clear that volunteers would not be enough to make up the losses. In January 1916, Parliament passed the first Conscription Act. This made military service compulsory for all single men between the ages of 18 and 41. Three months later, this was extended to include married men. Between 1916 and 1918, about one in three men were conscripted into the armed forces. Many people regarded conscription as fair. All men, in all sections of society, would have to share the burden and the risk of involvement in the fighting. It also meant that the Government could control which men, from which occupations, were called up. In this way, vital work, like mining, could still be conducted properly and efficiently.

Conscientious objectors

There were men who, for religious or humanitarian reasons, could not even begin to contemplate the awfulness of killing another human being. These conscientious objectors had to convince a tribunal that their reasons were genuine and not simple cowardice. Once convinced, a tribunal could order a conscientious objector to take part in non-combatant service at the Front, such as driving ambulances, or essential war work in Britain, such as mining or forestry. Men who refused to have anything at all to do with the war effort were imprisoned or sent to labour camps. Tribunals that did not accept a conscientious objector's case could order him into the army. If the man then refused to take orders, as many did, he was court-martialled and could be shot. Few people at the time had any sympathy for conscientious objectors. Their nickname 'conchies' was used derisively and the authorities took a dim view of them.

● **SOURCE 3**

Four of the many recruiting posters used during the First World War.

Why did men join up?

Men volunteered to fight in the armed services for many different reasons. Some were persuaded by the recruiting posters; others wanted to get away from a dead end job, their families or their wives; some wanted a share in the excitement; some thought it was their duty.

● **SOURCE 4**

A military band and marching soldiers are always an inspiring sight, but this was for real – they were off to war and how we youngsters envied them. And to tell you the truth, that was it – glamour – to be in uniform – to take part in a great adventure was as much the reason for so many youths joining up as was any sense of patriotism.

A man explains why, as a schoolboy, he wanted to join up.

● **SOURCE 5**

I was working in the colliery and there were people joining up, you know, and I thought, oh well – my brother-in-law, we discussed it and we decided to join up. We thought, well, a holiday, maybe, you know, that's what we thought. We'd beat the Germans in about six months. That's what we thought.

Irving Jones, a miner from south Wales, explains why he joined up.

● **SOURCE 6**

I feel I am to take an active part in this war. It is to me a very fascinating thing, something if often horrible, yet very ennobling and very beautiful.

Roland Leighton explains to Vera Brittain, the girl to whom he is engaged, why he has volunteered to fight.

● **SOURCE 7**

Many of the more mature men felt a genuine patriotism. There was an intense pride in Britain and the Empire and a general dislike of the Germans. The younger men were almost certainly inspired by the thoughts of adventure and travel at a time when few people had been further than their own city or the nearest seaside resort. The miners, industrial workers and unemployed often saw the call as a means of escape from their dismal conditions, away from slums and large families and into a new life where there was fresh air and good companionship, regular meals and all the glamour of Kitchener's Army.

From Martin Middlebrook, *The First Day on the Somme*, published in 1971.

Task

1 Look at Source 3 on page 55. How is each poster trying to persuade men to join up?
2 How does the appeal of the recruiting posters (Source 3) differ from that of the Kitchener poster (Source 1, page 53)?
3 What different reasons do Sources 4–6 give for men volunteering to fight?
4 In what ways do Sources 4–6 support what Martin Middlebrook is saying in Source 7?
5 Now look at Source 2 on page 54 and read the caption. What were the advantages and disadvantages of recruiting young men into Pals' Battalions?

Shells, bombs and threats of invasion

This war was not only fought far away in the battlefields of France, Belgium, Turkey and Palestine. For the first time, the destruction and violence of war was brought home, to mainland Britain. This was total war.

- **Shelling from the sea** In December 1914, German battleships shelled towns along the north-east coast of Britain. They shelled Scarborough, Whitby and Hartlepool, where 119 men, women and children were killed.
- **Zeppelins** In January 1915, German airships began bombing raids on Britain. These great, silver, cigar-shaped Zeppelins were 200 metres long and could carry 27 tonnes of bombs. Starting with Great Yarmouth and King's Lynn on the east coast, Zeppelins made a total of 57 raids on British towns, killing 564 people and injuring 1370.
- **Gotha and Giant bombers** In May 1917, German Gotha bombers raided Folkestone and killed 95 people. The following month, bombers raided London, killing 162 people including 16 children who died when their school was hit. All in all, the Germans made 27 bomber raids on British towns, causing a total of 835 deaths and over 1990 injuries.

● **SOURCE 8**

A photograph of Bartholomew Close, off Aldersgate Street, in the City of London, on the morning after the Zeppelin raid of 8 September 1915.

● **SOURCE 9**

The Zepp raid early Friday morning was a fine sight and we all much enjoyed it. It was rather cloudy and the searchlights showed up magnificently – scores of great beams sailing about the sky among the brilliant flashes of bursting shells, to the accompaniment of the sharp boom of the guns and the shorter crash of exploding shells, varied occasionally by the tremendous report of the Zepp bombs, which even at this distance of a good many miles made the hut shake.

Archie Steavenson, a young cadet in the Army Service Corps, describes a Zeppelin raid on the East End of London in August 1916.

Death and destruction brought by enemy action to mainland Britain showed that anyone and everyone was now at risk, regardless of their age, sex or role in society.

The shelling and bombing of east coast towns made many people fear that there was a very strong likelihood that the Germans were preparing an invasion force. The attacks on coastal towns had been a surprise and the Government had reacted by installing searchlights and setting up anti-aircraft guns and barrage balloons. The authorities were not going to be taken by surprise by an invasion. Detailed, highly secret instructions were prepared and sent to military commanders on the east coast. When the threat of invasion was over, all these instructions were handed back, still in their sealed envelopes, and were destroyed. By mistake, an extra copy of the instructions was mislaid.

● **SOURCE 11**

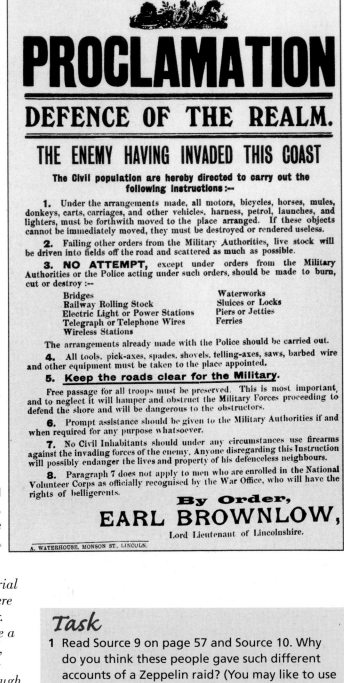

This secret proclamation was issued to all local military commanders along the east coast. It was not dated and was never issued to the general public.

● **SOURCE 10**

In an empty building plot, what was called an Aerial Torpedo had made not a hole but a crater, and there was evidence over a large area of its terrible power. One row of unfinished houses looked mixed up like a house of cards, windows everywhere were smashed, tiles and slates blown off and the side of the house facing the crater had a number of holes right through it and looked as though cannon balls had used it as a target. You can imagine the language of the East Enders who crowded here to see the damage, some in motors, costers' carts etc. down to the humble donkey.

A school teacher, Robert Saunders, describes, in a letter to his son, the effects of a Zeppelin raid on London in September 1916.

Task

1 Read Source 9 on page 57 and Source 10. Why do you think these people gave such different accounts of a Zeppelin raid? (You may like to use Source 7 on page 56 in your answer.)

2 Read Source 11. The proclamation is telling people what to do in the event of an invasion.
  a) How sensible are the instructions?
  b) Why do you think the proclamation was not issued in advance of an invasion so that people could be prepared?

How was Britain organised for war?

It was one thing to make sure there were enough men in the armed services to fight a war that was likely to last for several years. But that was only part of the problem. The Government had to find ways of using the nation's population to keep the country's economy going so that troops would be supplied and the people fed.

On 8 August 1914, Parliament passed the first of many Defence of the Realm Acts, nicknamed DORA. These Acts gave the Government power to bypass Parliament and issue directives that had the force of law. This meant that the Government could control almost every aspect of people's lives. The Government could, for example, order the seizure of land and buildings, take over industries vital to the war economy, and control information given to the public.

Controlling industry

- **Mining** One of the first things the Government did was to take control of the coal industry so that it could be run for the benefit of the war effort and not the coal owners. Their profits were fixed and the Treasury took any surplus. Miners were not conscripted into the armed forces because they were doing vital work. National wage agreements were made so that all miners, everywhere, were paid the same.
- **Munitions** In 1915, the *Daily Mail* newspaper exposed a munitions crisis which became a national scandal. It discovered that there was a chronic shortage of shells, bullets and guns on the Western Front. The munitions industry simply could not keep up and demand far outpaced supply. The Government set up a Ministry of Munitions, under the control of David Lloyd George, to increase the production of armaments. New National Shell factories were built, existing munitions factories controlled and their output co-ordinated. The latest machinery and mass-production methods were introduced throughout the industry by the Ministry, which also set wages and prices, and established new systems of financial control. In other words, the State controlled more than 20,000 munitions factories and those who worked in them.

● **SOURCE 12**

DELIVERING THE GOODS.

This cartoon was published in *Punch* magazine on 21 April 1915.

- **Railways** Railways were needed to move troops around the country, to and from training camps, and to ports from where they would be taken to the battle fronts. The Government took control of the railways and ran them as a single unified system. As with the mines, railway companies were guaranteed the same profit level they had had in 1913.
- **Shipping** When Lloyd George took over as Prime Minister in 1916, he set up a Ministry of Shipping. This requisitioned merchant ships for vital imports, co-ordinated the activities of docks and railways and increased the rate of construction of merchant ships. When German U-boats sank 3.7 million tonnes of British shipping in spring 1917, the Ministry of Shipping imposed a convoy system, whereby merchant ships sailed together, accompanied by battleships.

Controlling food production and distribution

By 1913, Britain was dependent on foreign food, importing 40 per cent of its meat, 80 per cent of its wheat, 50 per cent of its milk, fruit and vegetables and all of its sugar. As Britain is an island, these imports came by sea. During the war, an enemy with effective sea power could starve Britain to death. However, British sea power was so strong that supplies still got through from the Empire and the USA. The situation only became serious after the middle of 1916, when shortages occurred. In 1917, the situation became desperate because German U-boats were sinking one in four British merchant ships. By April 1917, Britain was down to nine weeks' supply of wheat and four days' supply of sugar. As food ran short, prices rose. Rich people bought more than they needed and hoarded it; the poor could not even afford basic foods like bread. Shops closed in the afternoons because they had run out of food.

David Lloyd George, the Prime Minister, tackled the problem in two ways:

Supply
- He set up a network of local committees whose job was to persuade farmers to turn their pasture land into arable land.
- By 1918, an additional 3 million acres of arable land had been brought into cultivation, wheat production had risen by 1 million tonnes and the potato crop by 1.5 million tonnes.

Demand
A Ministry of Food was set up which:

- subsidised the price of bread, which meant that the price of bread fell, and even the poorest families could buy as much as they needed. This was the 'ninepenny loaf'. The Government published posters encouraging people to eat less bread. But bread was never rationed and the subsidy kept its price down.
- set up local food committees which organised voluntary rationing. The Royal Family led the way by announcing that they were going to reduce the amount of bread they ate and flour used in the royal kitchens.
- introduced compulsory rationing. In 1918, sugar, meat, butter, jam and margarine were all rationed. This continued for some foods after the war; meat came off ration in November 1919, butter in early 1920 and sugar in November 1920.

● SOURCE 13

The Government was keen to persuade people to eat as little bread as possible, as these two posters, issued in 1917, show.

● **SOURCE 14**

DEFENCE OF THE REALM. E.P. 6.
MINISTRY OF FOOD.
BREACHES OF THE RATIONING ORDER
The undermentioned convictions have been recently obtained:—

Court	Date	Nature of Offence	Result
HENDON - -	29th Aug., 1918	Unlawfully obtaining and using ration books -	3 Months' Imprisonment
WEST HAM -	29th Aug., 1918	Being a retailer & failing to detach proper number of coupons	Fined £20
SMETHWICK -	22nd July, 1918	Obtaining meat in excess quantities - - -	Fined £50 & £5 5s. costs
OLD STREET -	4th Sept., 1918	Being a retailer selling to unregistered customer	Fined £72 & £5 5s. costs
OLD STREET -	4th Sept., 1918	Not detaching sufficient coupons for meat sold -	Fined £25 & £2 2s. costs
CHESTER-LE-STREET	4th Sept., 1918	Being a retailer returning number of registered customers in excess of counterfoils deposited - - -	Fined £50 & £3 3s. costs
HIGH WYCOMBE	7th Sept., 1918	Making false statement on application for and using Ration Books unlawfully - - - - - - -	Fined £40 & £6 4s. costs

Enforcement Branch, Local Authorities Division,
MINISTRY OF FOOD.
September, 1918.

There were enormous penalties for those who broke the rationing rules.

Business as usual?

In the early years of the war, people were determined to carry on as usual. East coast towns may have been bombed, casualties on the Western Front may have been mounting, but life in Britain had to go on as usual. In many ways this was praiseworthy; people's morale was kept high and their determination to win was strengthened. But in other ways, it was a disastrous attitude. 'Business as usual' meant eating as much as you wanted; it meant going on strike when you were dissatisfied with wartime wages and conditions; it meant getting drunk, going to work with a hangover and working less hard; and it meant gathering together in large crowds where the Germans could bomb and claim huge casualties. In other words, 'business as usual' had the potential to destroy the war effort.

In a series of keynote speeches in 1915, David Lloyd George, who was to become Prime Minister and war leader the following year, attacked the idea of 'business as usual'. He attacked, too, 'enjoyment as usual', and bitterly criticised wild parties, 'sprees' and the crowds who flocked to football matches and the theatre. He denounced alcohol, persuaded the King to set an example by giving it up altogether and restricted pub opening hours. Lloyd George used DORA to great effect. Bank Holidays, Guy Fawkes' night, the football league, race meetings and the Oxford and Cambridge boat race were cancelled, suspended or postponed.

Task

1 Why was DORA necessary?
2 Look at Source 12 on page 59. What point is the cartoonist making? Is the cartoonist in favour of the actions taken by Lloyd George?
3 Why was the Government so keen to stop people from eating too much bread? Use Source 13 and the information in this section in your answer.
4 Read Source 14. Why do you think the penalties for breaking the rules on rationing were so strict?
5 Why did Lloyd George try to destroy the idea of 'business as usual'? Do you think he was right to do so?

Women at war

The First World War transformed the position of women in society. During this time, women showed that they could do the jobs of men in the workplace and run a home and family as well. Even though most women were expected to return to a purely domestic role when the men came back, the image and the reality of women tram drivers and laboratory assistants, munitions workers, police officers and house painters could not be forgotten. The way to careers beyond the home had been opened. As you have seen in Unit 2, the war work of women was one of the factors that gained them the vote at the end of the war.

Supporting the men

The Government made it clear from the beginning of the war that the duty of men was to volunteer to fight for king and country. The duty of women was far from clear. At first, the Government thought little further than emphasising the role of women as supporters of men. They should encourage men to volunteer for the armed services, and they should run family firms and businesses while the men were away fighting.

● **SOURCE 15**

● **SOURCE 16**

A married woman takes over her husband's business, sticking up posters while he is away fighting.

An early government recruiting poster.

Filling the gaps

By the summer of 1915, this was not enough. Industry, particularly munitions, was desperately short of workers. Food, clothing and armaments had to be provided for fighting men. The obvious answer was to recruit women to fill the gaps, but this was not straightforward.

Male trade unionists were opposed to the employment of unskilled men in jobs that before the war had been reserved for skilled men. Trade unionists extended this attitude to women. They did not want to see women taking men's places, particularly in industry. Women were paid less than men, and the unions were afraid that, when the men returned from the war, the bosses would either pay them less or keep the women on instead of the men.

The munitions crisis brought matters to a head. It was vital that the munitions factories produced the armaments needed by the men at the Front, and to do this the way had to be cleared for the employment of women on a large scale.

Eventually, most of the trade unions made agreements with the Government or the employers that protected the men's jobs and wages. Most of these agreements stated that women should be paid the same as men and that the men could have their jobs back when they came home from the war.

It is important not to exaggerate the changes brought about by the war. There were important changes in the employment of women, but these were limited. In July 1914, nearly five million women were in employment. By the end of the war, this had gone up to just over six million. Source 18 shows that women gradually left domestic service. There were big increases in the number of women in munitions factories, banking and commerce, and metal-working jobs. The Women's Land Army was established to make sure that enough food was produced, but only 16,000 women joined. Most of the work on the farms was done by women already living in rural villages.

● SOURCE 17

David Lloyd George gave Emmeline Pankhurst a grant of £2000 from the Ministry of Munitions to organise a suffragette-style rally with the slogan 'Women's Right to Serve'. Lloyd George and Churchill addressed the rally, which attracted enormous publicity. This is a photograph of the gathering, which took place on 17 July 1915.

● SOURCE 18

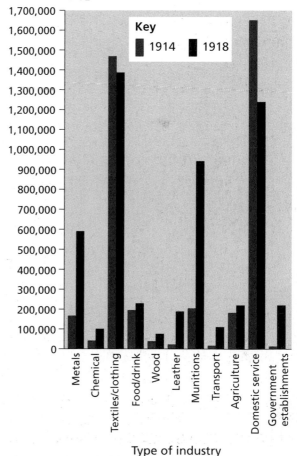

Type of industry

Employment figures for women, 1914 and 1918.

● **SOURCE 19**

An official war painting of women working in a munitions factory.

● **SOURCE 20**

A photograph of women working in a munitions factory.

Task

1 Do you think Sources 19 and 20 give different impressions of what it was like to work in a munitions factory? If so, why?

SOURCE 21

A photograph of women tar sprayers resurfacing a road.

SOURCE 22

A photograph of women police officers being inspected in 1915. The officer on the left had been a suffragette.

SOURCE 23

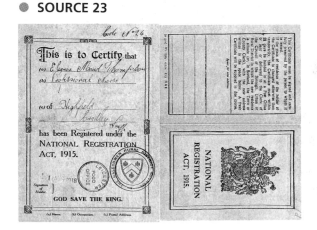

In August 1915, all men and women between the ages of 16 and 65 had to register their personal details so that the Government knew who was available for work. This is a National Registration Act certificate.

Recruiting women

As the war ground on and casualties rose, there was a switch to positively encouraging women to work full time. There was direct government persuasion to encourage women to join the Women's Land Army and to join the armed services as nurses, cooks, mechanics and drivers.

SOURCE 24

Government posters aimed at persuading women to join up.

The floodgates were open. Women did not only move into the work the Government wanted them to do. They worked as lathe operators and laboratory assistants, blacksmiths and air mechanics, nurses and orderlies, dentists and road sweepers, railway porters and foresters – any job, in fact, for which there was a vacancy.

Running home and family

Many women had to balance working outside the home with running a home and caring for children.

- **Food problems** The price of basic foodstuffs doubled during the war, and some items, like margarine, potatoes, meat, sugar and tea, became very scarce. How could women, tired out from working away from home, cope with shopping and cooking? Cheap restaurants sprung up, and the Government set up a string of national kitchens, where women could buy hot meals and take them home to eat.

● **SOURCE 25**

Food shortages meant that women spent many hours queuing for what was available, as shown in this photograph. Working women sent their children to queue; upper-class women sent their servants.

- **Rent strikes** Many landlords put up their rents so that they could make money from the newly recruited munitions and other factory workers. Women resisted this by organising a series of demonstrations and rent strikes. By October 1915 in Glasgow, for example, about 15,000 Clydeside tenants were refusing to pay and marched to the city hall. The situation looked dangerous and likely to spread to other cities. Rapidly, the Government passed the Rent Restriction Act, which kept rents at their 1913 level.
- **Separation allowances** The Government paid a weekly sum to the wives and dependents of all servicemen. If the man was killed, the allowance was turned into a pension. The amount of separation allowance depended on the rank of the serviceman and how many children he had.
- **Motherhood** Towards the end of the war, newspapers and magazines began to encourage the idea of motherhood. In 1916, Mother's Day was introduced to emphasise the value to the nation of its mothers; a National Baby Week was held in July 1917 with another one the following year. The National Council for the Unmarried Mother and her Child was founded – a sure sign that attitudes toward illegitimacy were changing.

● **SOURCE 26**

NATIONAL BABY WEEK

JULY 1st—7th, 1917.

President
THE RT. HON. DAVID LLOYD GEORGE.

Chairman of the Council
THE RT. HON. LORD RHONDDA.

Vice-Chairman of the Council : THE HON. WALDORF ASTOR, M.P.

Chairman of the Executive Committee : DR. ERIC PRITCHARD.

Vice-Chairman of the Executive Committee : MRS. A. C. GOTTO.

Hon. Secretary : MISS WRENCH.

Hon. Treasurer : W. HARDY, ESQ.

Secretary : MISS ALICE ELLIOTT.

SAVE THE BABIES

RE-BUILD THE NATION AND EMPIRE

"The Race marches forward on
the feet of Little Children."

**NATIONAL BABY WEEK,
KINGSWAY HOUSE,
KINGSWAY.
W.C. 2.**

TELEPHONE: REGENT 1890.

This poster is advertising the first National Baby Week, July 1917.

Social freedom

Women were more financially independent during the war than they had been before. Single women had their own money and married women, with or without children, were expected to manage their household budgets without any male input. Women began going to restaurants and pubs by themselves; they shortened their skirts and some began to smoke in public. Many people, particularly magistrates and churchmen, disapproved of this sort of behaviour. Indeed, pubs in Hartlepool refused to serve women at all.

The spread of sexually transmitted diseases (STDs) amongst soldiers and sailors was another problem that alarmed the authorities. Many towns tried to put a curfew on all women 'of a certain sort' between 7pm and 8am, despite outraged protests from 'respectable' women. Finally, the Government issued Regulation 40D, which said that if a woman infected a serviceman with an STD, she would be imprisoned. On the other hand, if a soldier or a sailor with an STD infected a woman, he would not be prosecuted.

Task

1 Look at Source 15 on page 62. What can you learn from this about the Government's attitude to women? Now look at Source 24 on page 65. How has this attitude changed? Use the information in this section to explain why the Government's attitude changed.

2 Look at Source 17 on page 63 and read the caption carefully. Look back to pages 40–42. Are you surprised that David Lloyd George should work with Emmeline Pankhurst in this way?

3 What do you consider to have been the most difficult problem faced by women during the First World War? Use the sources and information in this section to explain your answer.

4 Why do you think that, as the war drew to its end, there was a growing emphasis on the importance of motherhood?

Death

During the war, all people lived with the fear of death. Nearly 750,000 men were killed and thousands more injured. Most of the men who died were aged between 18 and 25 and each death brought tragedy to their families and friends.

The War Office notified the next of kin by telegram or by ordinary post that their son, husband or father had been killed, reported missing, or was a prisoner of war. As casualties mounted, standard letter forms were used to do this. If a family was lucky, their relative's commanding officer or a fellow serviceman would write a more personal note.

● **SOURCE 27**

This is the standard Army Form B 104–82B. It was sent with a formal message of sympathy from the King and Queen.

● **SOURCE 28**

I can remember my mother going pale one afternoon as she saw the telegram boy coming toward the house. She turned to me and smiled as he cycled past, but she didn't say a word. My father and brother were in the navy, and you never knew if the telegram was for you.

A woman remembers the tension her mother was under during the war.

● **SOURCE 29**

Dear Father
I am just writing you a short note which you will receive only if anything has happened to me in the next few days. The Hun is going to get terrible hell just in this quarter as we are going over the parapet tomorrow when I hope to spend a few merry hours chasing the Bosch all over the place. I am absolutely certain that I shall get through all right, but in case the unexpected does happen, I shall rest content with the knowledge that I have done my duty – and one can't do more.
Goodbye and with the best of love to all
From

Percy

This letter is from Second Lieutenant Percy Boswell to his father. He wrote it just before the Battle of the Somme in 1916. Percy was one of Kitchener's Volunteers who had joined the 8th King's Own Yorkshire Light Infantry. His battalion consisted of 774 men and 26 officers. They were part of the first wave of attack in the Battle of the Somme, 1916, and 21 officers and 518 men from the battalion were killed. Percy died in the first few minutes of the attack.

How effective was government propaganda during the war?

All governments use propaganda during war, and the British Government was no different. But what is propaganda and why do governments need to use it? Propaganda is limited, often biased, information used for a specific purpose. In times of war, this purpose is usually to keep up morale, to encourage people to support the war effort, and to create hatred and suspicion of the enemy. Propaganda also involves the control of information and censorship.

Newspaper reports

The role of the press during the war was crucial because newspapers were the public's main source of information. If newspapers did not print the truth, then people could not make an accurate assessment of events. If newspapers did print the truth, then there would probably be a collapse of morale, a fall in recruitment, possible mutiny in the armed forces, and strikes and rebellion at home. What was to be done?

At the start of the war, newspaper correspondents were not allowed at the Front at all. The Government gave newspapers a summary of what was happening. Early in the war, the British press did not report bad news. No casualty lists were published in newspapers until May 1915.

As the war progressed, specific language was used to keep morale high:

- a baptism of fire = heavy casualties
- rectification of the line = a retreat
- broken heroes = shell-shocked soldiers
- wastage = death

In fact, few people were killed; they 'fell', 'made the final sacrifice' or were 'slaughtered by the Hun'.

● SOURCE 30

I have seen – alas – many and have talked with some two scores of wounded soldiers, and I have not met one whose voice did not ring true and whose eyes, even in his pain, were not alight with the fire of triumph. They laughed as they told me about their own bit in the great fight; they showed by their bearing that they knew they had behaved well in front of their comrades.

A journalist reports interviews he has had with wounded soldiers. This is part of what was published in *The Times* on 18 September 1916.

The problem with such reports was that, whilst they may have kept morale high at home, soldiers knew that they were wrong. They knew that men were blown apart, and that wounded men wept and screamed in agony. A gulf was created between what people at home thought the war was like and what the soldiers knew it was like. Because of this, many soldiers could not talk to their friends and family about their experiences, their hopes and their fears. They felt betrayed and abandoned by the people at home who believed the lies.

Posters, postcards and cartoons

The visual impact of posters and postcards, in the days before television, was tremendous. The Government exploited this to the full. In the first year of the war, between two and five million copies of 110 different posters were issued. Most of them were targeted at recruitment, and all of them avoided any explicit description of the war. Later posters were aimed at combating war-weariness by publicising the terrible deeds of the enemy and the heroism of British troops.

The Government produced a set of official postcards called 'Telling the Story'. They show scenes from a young soldier's home leave, telling his proud parents about the honour and glory of fighting. All the photographs were posed and were laughed at by soldiers.

● SOURCE 32

Two posters produced by the Government.

● SOURCE 31

Two postcards from 'Telling the Story'.

● SOURCE 33

A GREAT NAVAL TRIUMPH.

This cartoon from the magazine *Punch* was published in 1911.

Magazines like *Punch* helped fire hatred of the Germans and so helped to unite the British public against the enemy.

Official photographs and paintings

Professional photographers were given officer status and privileged access to battlefields. On the Western Front, Germany had an average of 50 official photographers and France had around 35; Britain had just four. In the early years of the war, British photographers were not allowed to photograph the dead and the dying.

The first official British war artists were appointed in 1916 and, at first, the Government expected them to contribute to the national propaganda machine. However, when Lord Beaverbrook became Minister of Information in 1917, he was far more interested in collecting a record of the war, and both artists and photographers were allowed to work more freely.

Official films

There were many propagandist political cartoons made during the war and shown at cinemas across Britain. They aimed to persuade people to contribute to the war effort by mocking the Germans and by praising the efforts of Britain in facing the 'foe'.

● **SOURCE 34**

These images are from a cartoon film called *Britain's Effort*, made in 1918.

Perhaps the most well-known film to be made during the First World War was *The Battle of the Somme*. It was shown to British audiences, to the Royal Family at a private viewing, and to soldiers on the Western Front.

● **SOURCE 35**

We went on Wednesday night to a private view. I'm glad I went. I am glad I have seen the sort of thing our men have to go through, even to the sortie from the trench and the falling on barbed wire. There were pictures, too, of the battlefield after the fight, and of our gallant men lying all crumpled and helpless.

Frances Stevenson, David Lloyd George's secretary, writing about the film, *The Battle of the Somme*.

The Battle of the Somme (the real one) began on 1 July 1916 and lasted until November of the same year. The film version was showing in British cinemas by the second half of August 1916, long before the outcome of the real battle was known. What was going on here? It now seems that, although the preliminary bombardment and the march of battalions to front-line trenches were filmed on the Somme, the shots of the actual battle were taken miles away, probably at a trench mortar training school.

● **SOURCE 36**

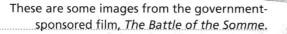

These are some images from the government-sponsored film, *The Battle of the Somme.*

Task

1 Read Source 30 on page 69 and look at Source 31 on page 70. Thousands of soldiers knew that these images of war were wrong. Why, then, were they produced? Use the information in this section to explain whether they did more harm than good.

2 Look at Source 32 on page 70. Now look back at the recruitment posters on page 55. Can you find any differences between them?

3 Read Source 35 on page 71 and look at Source 36.
   a) Why do you think the Government wanted this film made?
   b) Do you think it was effective propaganda?

4 Use the sources and information in this section to explain which propaganda items you found most effective.

Part 2
Source investigations

Why did the Liberal Government (1906–1912) decide to fight poverty?

Read all the sources, then answer the questions on page 76.

The Liberal Government elected, in 1906, began a series of welfare reforms. Within five years, Acts of Parliament were in place to take the elderly and children, the sick and the unemployed out of poverty. Yet these reforms had not even been mentioned in the Liberal Party's election manifesto. What were the motives that drove these reforms?

● **SOURCE A**

A photograph of slum housing in Liverpool, around 1900.

● **SOURCE B**

Under the window facing the door is the large bed, in which sleep mother, father and two children. A baby is asleep in a pram by the bed and another child is asleep in a cot in the corner. The second window can be, and is, left partly open at night. At the foot of the bed is a small table. Three wooden chairs and a chest of drawers complete the furniture. The small fireplace has no oven, and open shelves go up each side of it. There are two saucepans, both burnt. There is no larder.

From *Round about a Pound a Week* by Maud Pember Reeves, published in 1913. She is describing a room in Lambeth, south London, lived in by one family in the early years of the twentieth century.

● **SOURCE C**

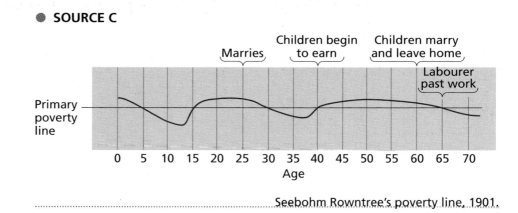

Seebohm Rowntree's poverty line, 1901.

● **SOURCE D**

We were challenged by the member for Preston who said 'Would you declare that you are in favour of giving a pension of 5s a week to a drunken, thriftless, worthless man or woman?' My reply is very prompt. A man of seventy with nothing in the world is going to cut a pretty shine on 5s a week, whether his character be good or bad. Who are you, to be continually finding fault? Who amongst you has such a clear record as to be able to point to the wickedness of an old man of seventy? If a man is foolish enough to get old, and if he has not been artful enough to get rich, you have no right to punish him for it.

Will Crooks MP (1852–1921) describes his attitude to old age pensions. He was the first person born in a workhouse to become an MP.

● **SOURCE E**

THE BIG DOG AND THE LITTLE ONE.

LORD HALSBURY: I don't think much of that paltry little thing—it's a mockery of a dog.

AGED PENSIONER: Well, my lord, 'tis only a little 'un, but 'tis a wunnerful comfort to me. Us bain't all blessed wi' big 'uns!

A Liberal Party leaflet, published 1 February 1909.

● **SOURCE F**

THE DAWN OF HOPE.

Mr. LLOYD GEORGE'S National Health Insurance Bill provides for the insurance of the Worker in case of Sickness.

Support the Liberal Government
in their policy of
SOCIAL REFORM.

This cartoon, 'The Dawn of Hope', was published in 1911.

● **SOURCE G**

Number of Labour and Liberal MPs elected in general elections 1900–18

Key
■ Labour
■ Liberal

Labour: 1900: 2, 1906: 29, 1910 Jan: 40, 1910 Dec: 42, 1918: 57

Liberal: 1900: 183, 1906: 399, 1910 Jan: 274, 1910 Dec: 272, 1918: 163

Percentage of votes won by the Labour Party and Liberal Party in general elections 1900–18

Key
■ Labour
■ Liberal

Labour: 1900: 1.3, 1906: 4.8, 1910 Jan: 7.0, 1910 Dec: 6.4, 1918: 20.8

Liberal: 1900: 45.0, 1906: 49.4, 1910 Jan: 43.5, 1910 Dec: 44.2, 1918: 25.6

Voting figures in general elections 1900–18.

● **SOURCE H**

FORCED FELLOWSHIP.

Suspicious-looking Party. "ANY OBJECTION TO MY COMPANY, GUV'NOR? I'M AGOIN' YOUR WAY"—(aside) "AND FURTHER."

This cartoon, called 'Forced Fellowship', was published in *Punch* magazine in 1909.

Questions

1 Study **Source A**.
What does this source tell you about poverty at the beginning of the twentieth century? [6]

2 Study **Sources B** and **C**.
Is one source more reliable than the other to a historian studying poverty at the beginning of the twentieth century?
Use the sources and your own knowledge in your answer. [9]

3 Study **Sources D** and **E**.
How far do these sources differ in their attitude to old age pensions?
Use the sources and your own knowledge in your answer. [9]

4 Study **Source F**.
Why was this poster issued in 1911?
Use the source and your own knowledge in your answer. [6]

5 Study **Sources G** and **H**.
How far does Source G support the message of Source H?
Use the sources and your own knowledge in your answer. [8]

6 Study **all** the sources and use your own knowledge.
'The Liberal Party introduced welfare reforms only because they were afraid of the rise of the Labour Party.'
Explain whether or not you agree with this interpretation. [12]

How important were the Liberal social reforms?

**Read all the sources,
then answer the
questions on
page 79.**

The social reforms of 1906–12 were aimed at helping the old, the poor, the sick, the unemployed and children. Some historians have claimed that these reforms only helped a few people in a limited way. Others have claimed that they made a real difference. Just as importantly, they argue that these reforms introduced the idea that the State had a responsibility to those in need and that they laid the foundations of the Welfare State.

● SOURCE A

The Old Age Pensions Act is just the beginning of things. We are still confronted with the more gigantic task of dealing with the sick, the infirm, the unemployed, the widows and the orphans. No country can be called civilised that allows them to starve. Starvation is a punishment that society has ceased to inflict for centuries on its worst criminals, and at its most barbarous stage humanity never starved the children of the criminal.

I have had some excruciating letters piled upon me from people whose cases I have investigated – honest workmen thrown out of work, tramping the streets from town to town begging for work, and at the end of the day trudging home tired, disheartened, and empty handed, to be greeted by faces, and some of them little faces, haggard and pinched with starvation and anxiety. During years of prosperity the workman has helped to create the enormous piles of wealth that have accumulated in the country. Surely, a few of these millions might be spared to preserve from hunger the workmen who have helped to make that great wealth.

David Lloyd George speaking in October 1908.

● SOURCE B

There were one or two poorer couples, just holding on to their homes, but in daily fear of the workhouse. When the Old Age Pensions began, life was transformed for such aged cottagers. They were relieved of anxiety. They were suddenly rich. Independent for life! At first, when they went to the Post Office to draw it, tears of gratitude would run down the cheeks of some, and they would say as they picked up their money, 'God bless that Lloyd George!' (for they could not believe one so powerful and munificent could be a plain 'Mr.')

An extract from *Lark Rise to Candleford* by Flora Thompson, a book of memoirs of living in a country village in the early twentieth century.

● SOURCE C

At last, in 1908, the Liberal Government allocated £1,200,000 for the establishment of a non-contributory old-age pension scheme, and an Act was passed to become law on 1 January 1909.

Pensions, however, would be withheld from those 'who had failed to work according to their ability and need, and those who had failed to save money regularly'. Here was a means test with a vengeance. Paupers were not entitled to any pension. Nevertheless, even these small doses meant life itself for many among the elderly poor. Old folk, my mother (who was a shopkeeper) said, spending their allowance at the shop, 'would bless the name of Lloyd George as if he was a saint from heaven'.

From Richard Roberts, *The Classic Slum*, published in 1973.

● SOURCE D

THE PHILANTHROPIC HIGHWAYMAN.

Mr. Lloyd-George. *"I'LL MAKE 'EM PITY THE AGED POOR!"*

A cartoon published in 1909. The figure shown as a highwayman is Lloyd George.

● SOURCE E

A cartoon published in 1911. The figure on the left is Lloyd George.

● SOURCE F

Dear Sir

The strength of this kingdom, in all its past struggles, has been its great reserve of wealth and the sturdy independent character of its people. The measure which is being pushed through the House of Commons with haste will destroy both. It will extort wealth from its possessors by unjust taxation. It will distribute it in small doles, the most wasteful of all forms of expenditure, and will weaken the character of the people by teaching them to rely, not on their own exertions, but on the State.

A letter to *The Times*, July 1908.

● SOURCE G

Ex-soldiers of 1914–18 too ill to work but some not entitled to pensions: men hurt in the pits, able at most for light work but no light work available and compensation being stopped. Women living in two-roomed cottages with one of the rooms so damp that the water ran down the wall and the whole family had to huddle together, sleeping and waking, day and night, when they were sick and when they were well, all in one apartment. Old people hungry because they could not spin out their ten-shilling pension to cover food and fuelling to the end of the week. Unemployed men in areas where no work was available cut off benefit for 'not genuinely seeking work'.

From *Tomorrow is a New Day* by Jennie Lee, published in 1939.

● SOURCE H

A cartoon published in 1909. The figure leaning over the table is Lloyd George.

● SOURCE I

Four spectres haunt the poor – old age, accident, sickness and unemployment. We are going to drive hunger from the hearth. We mean to banish the workhouse from the horizon of every workman in the land.

....Lloyd George speaking in the 1910 election campaign.

● SOURCE J

In relation to the size of the problem of poverty the Old Age Pensions Act was inadequate. The Government failed to carry out a complete reorganisation of the Poor Law. The emotional excitement which it was possible to generate on account of the Act is proof of how little the poor had come to expect of their rulers. Yet, for the aged poor it might make it easier to avoid the workhouse, and it was the beginning of the end of a social system based on the notion that the only way to keep the masses at work was the threat of starvation. There was also little progress in housing, town planning and public health.

They relieved the worst effects of poverty but two important criticisms have to be made. The reforms were limited – the pensions were very small, and paid only to the poorest; unemployment insurance covered only a small proportion of the workforce. Secondly, nothing was done about the Poor Law which survived until 1929. However, the Government had now been involved in helping the old, sick and poor; the foundations for the Welfare State had been laid.

....The recent judgement of an historian.

Questions

1 Study **Source A**.
How do you think Lloyd George made this speech in 1908?
Use the source and your own knowledge to explain your answer.   [6]

2 Study **Sources B** and **C**.
How far do these two sources agree?
Use the sources to explain your answer.   [6]

3 Study **Sources D** and **E**.
Are these two cartoonists supporting or criticising Lloyd George?
Use the sources and your own knowledge to explain your answer.   [8]

4 Study **Sources F** and **G**.
Does Source G prove that the writer of Source F was wrong?
Use the sources and your own knowledge to explain your answer.   [8]

5 Study **Source H**. (See also page 20.)
Why was this cartoon published in 1909?
Use the cartoon and your own knowledge to explain your answer.   [6]

6 Study **Sources I** and **J**.
Why do you think these two sources differ in the information they give about the reforms?
Use the sources and your own knowledge to explain your answer.   [6]

7 Study **all** the sources.
Do these sources show that the Liberal reforms were important?
Use the sources and your own knowledge to explain your answer.   [10]

Were the suffragettes justified in using violence?

Read all the sources, then answer the questions on page 82.

In 1908, the suffragettes turned to violence. At first, this consisted of window-breaking, but many other types of violent protest followed. To the suffragettes these methods were justified. They believed this was the only way they could make the Government take notice of them. They also claimed they were merely responding to the violence of the Government and the police. Many people at the time were horrified by the violent tactics; as far as they were concerned, this violence could not be justified. Others claimed that the tactics were making votes for women less, rather than more, likely.

● SOURCE A

Window-breaking began that night. It was the women's first use of the political argument of the stone. Mary Leigh and Edith New, taking counsel with no one, had gone to Downing Street carrying stones, and flung them at the windows of the Prime Minister's official abode. Defending this action in Court the next day, the two prisoners said that having tried every other means to achieve their end, and having failed, they had had to take more militant measures. The responsibility for what they have done rested on those who made women outlaws by the law of the land.

From *Unshackled* by Christabel Pankhurst, published in 1959. She is describing an incident in June 1908.

● SOURCE B

Window-breaking, when Englishmen do it, is regarded as an honest expression of political opinion. Window-breaking, when Englishwomen do it, is treated as a crime. In sentencing Mrs Leigh and Miss New to two months the magistrate used very severe language, and declared that such a thing must never happen again. Of course the women assured him it would happen again. Said Mrs Leigh: 'We have no other course but to rebel against oppression, and if necessary to resort to stronger measures. This fight is going on.'

An extract from *My Own Story* by Emmeline Pankhurst, published in 1914.

● SOURCE C

A photograph of three suffragettes about to chain themselves to the railings outside a government building in 1909.

● SOURCE D

No one surely can have imagined destruction on this scale in London. Until recently the suffragist militant section have at least been able to urge that only violent methods would secure from Parliament what they desire. But now not even that excuse remains. There is indeed, only one explanation for this crowning folly, which is not merely folly but crime – that the obvious movement of public opinion from indifference to hostility has reduced them to despair. Observers may perhaps feel that a demonstration which so utterly condemns its cause needs nothing but the passing pity we give to the insane.

Extract from *The Times*, March 1912.

● SOURCE E

On learning that Mr Asquith had shelved the Conciliation Bill it was decided to send a deputation to him. This deputation consisted of over 300 women. The treatment which this deputation received was the worst that has been meted out to any deputation since the conflict between women and the Government began. The orders of the Home Secretary were, apparently, that the police were to be present both in uniform and also in plain clothes among the crowd and that the women were to be thrown from one to the other. As a result, many women were severely hurt, and several were knocked down and bruised. Finally, one hundred and fifteen women were arrested.

An account of 'Black Friday', 18 November 1910, from *Votes for Women*, 25 November 1910. (*Votes for Women* was a suffragette journal.)

● SOURCE F

A photograph of some of the events of Black Friday.

● SOURCE G

For hours I was beaten about the body, thrown backwards and forwards from one to another, until one felt dazed with the horror of it. Often seized by the coat collar and pushed into a side street while the policeman beat up and down on my spine until cramp seized my legs, when he would release me with a vicious shove, and with insulting speeches, such as 'I will teach you a lesson. I will teach you not to come back any more. I will punish you, you-, you-'. Once I was thrown with my jaw against a lamp-post with such force that two of my front teeth were loosened.

One of the 150 statements made by suffragettes about the events on Black Friday.

● SOURCE H

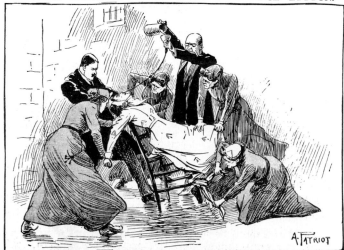

PRISON EXPERIENCES OF LADY CONSTANCE LYTTON.

FORCIBLE FEEDING IN PRISON.

From the front cover of *Votes for Women*, 28 January 1910.

● SOURCE I

It is almost impossible to write the story of the Women's Rebellion without admitting certain elements of brutal comedy. From the spectacle of women attacking men there arises laughter. And when a scene as ordinary as English politics is suddenly disturbed with the swish of long skirts, the violent assault of feathered hats, the advance of corseted bosoms – when, around the smoking ruins of some house or church, there is discovered the dreaded evidence of a few hairpins – then the amazing, the ludicrous appearance of the whole thing is almost irresistible.

From *The Strange Death of Liberal England* by George Dangerfield, a history book published in 1935.

● SOURCE J

In a Parliamentary sense, the movement has gone back. In the last two sessions we have been beaten, and you may depend upon it that, in a movement like this, Parliament represents the temporary mood of the nation. For the moment, the militants have created a situation which is the worst I have seen for women's suffrage in Parliament.

Lloyd George, speaking in October 1913.

● SOURCE K

Mrs Pankhurst said 'If the general public were pleased with what we are doing, that would be proof that our warfare is ineffective'. Yet, these tactics played into the hands of the politicians rather than increasing pressure on them. Ministers, including Lloyd George, insisted that by 1913 the militants had made the cause so unpopular in the country that nothing could be done. This of course must be seen for what it was – a convenient excuse.

From Martin Pugh, *The March of the Women*, published in 2000.

Questions

1   Study **Sources A** and **B**.
     How far do these two sources agree about why it was necessary for the suffragettes to turn to violence?
     Use the sources to explain your answer.   [6]

2   Study **Sources C** and **D**.
     Which of these two sources is most useful in explaining the methods used by the suffragettes?
     Use the sources and your own knowledge to explain your answer.   [8]

3   Study **Sources E, F** and **G**.
     Do these three sources prove beyond any doubt that the police treated the protesters with unjustified violence on Black Friday?
     Use the sources and your own knowledge to explain your answer.   [9]

4   Study **Source H**.
     Why do you think *Votes for Women* published this cartoon on its front cover in January 1910?
     Use the source and your own knowledge to explain your answer.   [8]

5   Study **Sources J** and **K**.
     Is Source J more reliable than Source K?
     Use the sources and your own knowledge to explain your answer.   [7]

6   Study **all** the sources.
     Do these sources show that the use of violence by the suffragettes was justified?
     Use the sources and your own knowledge to explain your answer. [12]

Was Emily Davison exploited by the suffragettes?

Read all the sources, then answer the questions on page 85.

On 4 June 1913, a suffragette called Emily Davison went to Epsom racecourse to watch the Derby. As the horses drew level with her, she slipped under the rails and threw herself at the King's horse, Anmer. The horse trampled her underfoot and she died shortly afterwards. The suffragettes gave her a magnificent public funeral, claiming that she had died for the cause of female suffrage. But had she? Was her death anything more than a tragic accident – a protest that went badly wrong? More importantly, did the suffragettes exploit her death for publicity purposes?

● **SOURCE A**

A photograph of Emily Davison at the Derby from *Lloyd's Weekly News*, 8 June 1913.

● **SOURCE B**

On her jacket being removed, I found two suffragette flags 1¹⁄₂ yards long by ³⁄₄ yard wide, each consisting of green, white and purple stripes folded up and pinned to the back of her jacket on the inside.
On her person was found:
1 purse containing three shillings and eightpence three farthings
1 return half of a railway ticket from Epsom to Victoria
2 postal orders for 2/6 and 7/6
8 postage stamps
1 key
1 Helper's Pass for the Suffragette Festival, Empress Rooms, High Street, Kensington, for 4 June 1913
1 memo book
1 race card
Some envelopes and writing paper
1 handkerchief.

Part of the official police report on the events surrounding the death of Emily Davison.

● **SOURCE C**

Emily Davison and a fellow-militant in whose flat she lived, had planned a Derby protest without tragedy – a mere waving of the purple-white-and-green at Tattenham Corner, which, by its suddenness, it was hoped would stop the race. Whether from the first her purpose was more serious, or whether a final impulse altered her resolve, I know not. Her friend declares that she would not thus have died without writing a farewell message to her mother. Yet, she sewed the WSPU colours inside her coat as though to ensure that no mistake could be made as to her motive when her body should be examined.

From Sylvia Pankhurst, *The Suffrage Movement: An Intimate Account of Persons and Ideals*, published in 1931.

● **SOURCE D**

The case will, of course, become the subject of investigation by the police and we may possibly learn from the offender herself, what exactly she intended to do and how she fancied it would help the suffragist cause. A deed of this kind, we need hardly say, is not likely to increase the popularity of any cause with the ordinary public. We believe that yesterday's exhibition had done more to hurt the cause of women's suffrage than to help it.

From *The Times*, 5 June 1913.

● **SOURCE E**

Mother was ill from her second hunger strike when there came the news of Emily Davison's historic act. She had stopped the King's horse at the Derby and was lying mortally injured. We were as startled as everyone else. Not a word had she said of her purpose. Taking advice from no one, she had gone to the racecourse, waited her moment and rushed forward. Horse and jockey were unhurt, but Emily Davison paid with her life for making the whole world understand that women were in earnest for the vote. Probably in no other way and at no other time and place could she so effectively have brought the concentrated attention of millions to bear upon the cause.

From Christabel Pankhurst, *Unshackled*, published in 1959.

● **SOURCE F**

Photograph of Emily Davison's funeral procession through London, 14 June 1913.

● **SOURCE G**

She was the first to talk about dying for the cause. Her suicide was a brave act, but foolish and unnecessary; it had little effect on the 'Votes for Women' movement, except to confirm for many that a sensible idea had become exaggerated out of all proportion.

From D C Brooks, *The Emancipation of Women*, published in 1970.

● **SOURCE H**

A cartoon from the *Daily Herald*, June 1913.

Questions

1 Study **Source A**.
What can you learn from this source about events at Tattenham Corner on the Derby racecourse on 4 June 1913? [6]

2 Study **Sources B** and **C**.
How far do these sources help explain whether or not Emily Davison's death was a suicide?
Use the sources and your own knowledge in your answer. [6]

3 Study **Sources D** and **E**.
Why do you think these two sources give such different reactions to the impact of Emily Davison's death?
Use the sources and your own knowledge in your answer. [9]

4 Study **Source F**.
How useful is this source to a historian trying to find out about the ways in which the suffragettes used Emily Davison's death?
Use the source and your own knowledge in your answer. [8]

5 Study **Sources G** and **H**.
Is one source more reliable than the other about attitudes to Emily Davison's death?
Use the sources and your own knowledge in your answer. [9]

6 Study **all** the sources and use your own knowledge.
'Emily Davison's death was a futile gesture that helped no one.'
How far would you agree with this interpretation? [12]

Women's war work: What did it achieve for women?

Read all the sources, then answer the questions on page 88.

On 4 August 1914, Great Britain declared war on Germany. Almost immediately, 500,000 men volunteered to join the regular British army of about 250,000 soldiers. By March 1916, 2.5 million men had left their peacetime jobs and were involved in the business of war. Women were involved in the business of war, too. They had to look after the homes and children the men had left behind. They had to drive trains, plough fields, clean street lamps, print newspapers, weld machinery, fight fires; everything the men had done. They also had to make bombs and bullets. Did they achieve anything through their presence in the workplace? Did the war change society's attitudes to women?

● **SOURCE A**

A poster issued by the Parliamentary Recruitment Committee in 1914.

● **SOURCE B**

A poster issued by the Government in 1916.

● **SOURCE C**

A poster issued by the Government in 1915.

● **SOURCE D**

Over and over again, the foreman gave me wrong or incomplete directions and altered them in such a way as to give me hours more work. I had no tools that I needed, and it was only on Saturdays that I could get to a shop. It was out of the question to borrow anything from the men. Two shop stewards informed me on the first day that they had no objection to my working there provided I received the full men's rate of pay. But after this, none of the men spoke to me for a long time, and would give me no help. My drawer was nailed up by the men, and oil was poured over everything in it through a crack the other night. Had I been satisfied that my work was good I should have been content, but I felt I had not sufficient skill to hold my own against an antagonistic foreman and decided I would give up.

Dorothy Poole speaks of her wartime experiences in a factory.

● **SOURCE E**

I could quite see it was hard on the men to have women going into all their pet jobs and in some cases doing them a good deal better. I sympathised with the way they were torn between not wanting the women to undercut them and yet hating them to earn as much.

Joan Williams, a munitions worker, remembers her factory experiences.

● **SOURCE F**

We, as women, also love the old tradition that the wife's place is in the home. But if we are going to be content with a woman's wage for a man's job, then we shall be serving not only our dear ones behind the guns and in the trenches, but their old enemies, the master classes who will be seeking cheap labour.

A trade union official remembers her wartime working experiences.

● **SOURCE G**

How could we have carried on the war without women? There is hardly a service in which women have not been at least as active as men. Wherever we turn we see them doing work which three years ago would have been regarded as being exclusively 'men's work'. But what moves me still more in this matter is the problem of what to do when the war is over. I would find it impossible to withhold from women the power and the right of making their voices directly heard.

Part of a speech made by Herbert Asquith to the House of Commons in 1917.

● **SOURCE H**

A Question of Presents

Q *I have been keeping company with a young man for about six months. His birthday comes first. Would it be correct for me to give him a small present?*

A *Give him a flower to put in the buttonhole of his coat. It would be unwise to give anything more valuable than that.*

'Perplexed May'   It is always a very risky thing for a girl to make the acquaintance of a man to whom she has not been introduced.

Returning the Engagement Ring

'Anxious'   No one can compel you to return the ring your former sweetheart gave you. I am afraid I must say you are well rid of him. A man who, having gone out with you for five years, can then demand the return of the ring, with threats of 'further trouble' if you don't give it up, is too contemptible for words. He will not make a good husband and you will be very foolish to break your heart over the business.

Extracts from the problem page of *Woman's Weekly* magazine, August 1918.

Questions

1   Study **Source A**.
    What can you learn from this source about attitudes to women in Britain in 1914?
    Use the source in your answer.   [6]

2   Study **Sources A** and **B**.
    Why do you think these posters make different appeals to women?
    Use the sources and your own knowledge in your answer.   [8]

3   Study **Source C**.
    Why was this poster produced in 1915?
    Use the source and your own knowledge in your answer.   [6]

4   Study **Sources D** and **E**.
    How far does Source E explain what was happening in Source D?
    Use the sources and your own knowledge in your answer.   [9]

5   Study **Sources F, G** and **H**.
    How useful are these sources to a historian studying changing attitudes to women during the First World War?
    Use the sources and your own knowledge in your answer.   [9]

6   Use **all** the sources and your own knowledge.
    'The First World War did nothing to change the status of women in British society.' How far would you agree with this statement?   [12]

Did the First World War help or hinder women getting the vote?

Read all the sources, then answer the questions on page 92.

It is often claimed that some women were granted the vote in 1918 as recognition for their contribution to the war effort. How far is this true? Some historians have claimed that the campaign for women to be granted the vote was gathering in strength in the years just before 1914, and that the war delayed the vote being granted. Others argue that the militant methods of the suffragettes made the public and the Government more determined not to grant women the vote and that it was only their work in the war that changed people's minds. Did the war help or hinder women being granted the vote?

● **SOURCE A**

The suffragists reacted with dismay to the resumption of militancy in 1912. The leaders of the WSPU rejected this. Flora Drummond reportedly declared that she 'cared not what the opinion of the public was as regards destroying letters'; Annie Kenney asked: 'what do we care whether we have public opinion with us or not?' Yet these tactics played into the hands of the politicians rather than increasing pressure on them. Government ministers insisted that by 1913 the militants had made the cause so unpopular in the country that nothing could be done. This of course must be seen for what it was – a convenient excuse. Yet it cannot simply be dismissed as an excuse, for the politicians' views appeared to be supported by the widespread attacks on the WSPU activists in public places.

From Martin Pugh, *The March of the Women*, published in 2000.

● **SOURCE B**

The violence offered by the suffragettes has not been formidable, and the fiercest of them have been far more ready to suffer pain than to inflict it.

What those endured who underwent the hunger strike and the anguish of force-feeding can hardly be overestimated. Their courage made a deep impression on the public.

Millicent Fawcett in 1911.

● **SOURCE C**

On Saturday the pilgrimage of the law-abiding advocates of 'votes for women' ended in a great gathering in Hyde Park attended by some 50,000 persons. The proceedings were quite orderly. They were, indeed, as much a demonstration against militancy as one in favour of women's suffrage. Many bitter things were said of the militant women.

An account of the Women's Pilgrimage reaching London in July 1913 from *The Times.*

● **SOURCE D**

Suffragette activity was at its greatest height. In the prisons heroic women were fighting, militants roved the country. Public meetings were held on a large scale. Suffragettes were everywhere, in everything, constantly surpassing themselves in service and sacrifice. After nearly nine years of increasing militancy the women were winning. The Government was getting very much afraid – of the loss of votes at the election and still more afraid of the women themselves. Then suddenly, the other war broke out!

From Christabel Pankhurst, *Unshackled*, published in 1959.

● **SOURCE E**

By 1912–14 the WSPU was in decline and becoming increasingly isolated from the rest of the women's movement. The key development in this period consists of the expansion of the National Union of Women's Suffrage Societies.

There are three important trends that explain the eventual outcome of the campaign. First, while militant suffragism was diminishing before 1914, suffragism as a whole expanded. Second, the movement was moving in the opposite direction to the WSPU. Third, suffragism began to cross the class barrier and to develop into something like a mass movement which was much more difficult for the Asquith Government to ignore. The war interrupted the process before the new strategy had been fully tested.

From Martin Pugh, *The March of the Women*, published in 2000.

● **SOURCE F**

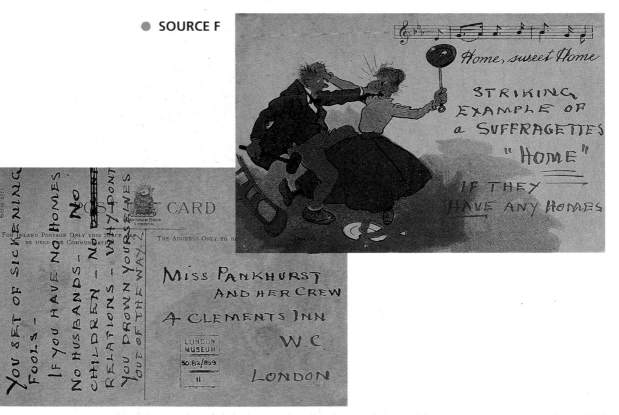

The front and back of one of the insulting postcards sent to the WSPU headquarters as the campaign became more militant.

● SOURCE G

I have had unlimited correspondence from every section of the public who have been good enough to advise me what to do, and among them I have not been able to discover more than four alternative methods. The first, is to let them die. That is, I should say, at the present moment, the most popular, judging by the number of letters I have received. The second is to deport them. The third is to treat them as lunatics, and the fourth is to give them the vote. I think we should not adopt any of them.

The Home Secretary, Reginald McKenna, speaking in the House of Commons in June 1914. As Home Secretary, he was the Government Minister responsible for law and order.

● SOURCE H

VOTES FOR HEROINES AS WELL AS HEROES

CHIVALRY: "Men and women protect one another in the hour of death. With the addition of the woman's vote, they would be able to protect one another in life as well."

A cartoon on the front cover of *Votes for Women*, November 1915.

● SOURCE I

The women who did most of the war work were young, single and working class. The politicians had no intention of letting them dominate politics. The government saw them as unstable, too much of an unknown quantity. They were much happier with the older, married, family women who had done less in the war and were not after jobs in industry – and who would probably vote exactly as their husbands did. It was these women who got the vote in 1918.

Martin Pugh, modern historian.

● **SOURCE J**

How could we have carried on the war without women? There is hardly a service in which women have not been at least as active as men. Wherever we turn we see them doing work which three years ago we would have regarded as being exclusively 'men's work'. But what moves me still more in this matter is the problem of what to do when the war is over. I would find it impossible to withhold from women the power and the right of making their voices directly heard.

And let me add that, since the war began, now nearly three years ago, we have had no repeat of that detestable campaign which disfigured the political history of this country, and no one can now contend that we are yielding to violence what we refused to concede to argument.

Herbert Asquith speaking in Parliament in 1917.
(He lost his job as Prime Minister in 1916.)

Questions

1   Study **Source A**.
    What is the author's view of the suffragettes?
    Use the source to explain your answer.   [5]

2   Study **Sources B** and **C**.
    Is there any reason to be surprised by Source C after reading what
    Source B has to say?
    Use the sources and your own knowledge to explain your answer.   [8]

3   Study **Sources D** and **E**.
    Do these two sources disagree more than they agree?
    Use the sources to explain your answer.   [6]

4   Study **Sources F** and **G**.
    How far do these two sources prove that the suffragettes were very
    unpopular by 1914?
    Use the sources and your own knowledge to explain your answer.   [7]

5   Study **Source H**.
    In what ways is this source useful to a historian studying the campaign
    for votes for women?
    Use the source and your own knowledge to explain your answer.   [7]

6   Study **Sources I** and **J**.
    Does Source I mean that Asquith was lying in Source J?
    Use the sources and your own knowledge to explain your answer.   [7]

7   Study **all** the sources.
    Do these sources prove that the war hindered, rather than helped,
    women win the vote?
    Use the sources and your own knowledge to explain your answer.   [10]

How effective was government propaganda during the First World War?

Read all the sources, then answer the questions on page 97.

During the First World War, it was crucial that men joined the armed forces in large numbers and that public morale was kept high. It is often claimed that government propaganda was very successful in achieving these aims. Yet some historians claim that government propaganda was not that effective and that other factors were responsible for keeping the British people behind the war effort.

SOURCE A

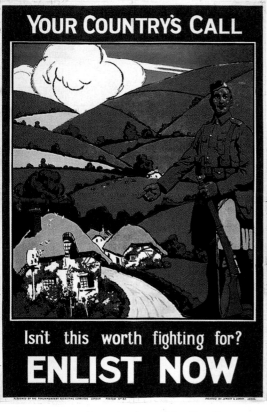

A poster issued by the Government.

SOURCE B

A poster issued by the Government.

● **SOURCE C**

A poster issued by the Government.

● **SOURCE D**

A chaotic approach to propaganda reigned until the last year of the war. Most of the morale-boosting was carried out unconsciously by ordinary citizens. Even at the worst of times, the vast majority of the population wanted to believe that the war was proceeding well. The most popular rumours were those which inspired optimism, such as stories of an angel strengthening the British line at Mons, and of Russian soldiers (still with snow on their boots) seen throughout Britain in August 1914.

The MP Stanley Baldwin admitted that, 'Propaganda is not a word that has a pleasant sound in English ears'. A wartime memo from a government office commented that government advertising 'was thought to be useless'.

Much praise has been given to British propaganda for its contribution to victory, but one doubts that it was responsible for encouraging people at home towards greater effort. The most valuable propaganda work was done inadvertently by the Germans. They were very good at appearing evil, a fact which impressed the British people more than the constant messages about the worthiness of their own cause.

From G J Degroot, *Blighty: British society in the Era of the Great War*, published in 1996.

● **SOURCE E**

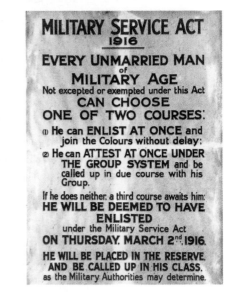

A poster issued in 1916 announcing conscription.

● **SOURCE F**

In 1916 with the knowledge that the war would not be a short one there was increasing pressure for more volunteers. Recruitment sergeants interrupted cinema shows with grisly descriptions of German brutality, of the killing of women and children for the fun of it, and in the war hysteria of the day we believed it. The truth is we wanted to believe it. The most effective recruiting agents, however, were the women and girls who handed out white feathers to men not in uniform and not wearing a war service badge.

From W H A Groom, *Poor Bloody Volunteers*, the memoirs of a First World War soldier.

● **SOURCE G**

In 1914 I was just an ordinary boy of elementary education and poor prospects. Rumours of war broke out and I began to be interested in the Territorials tramping the streets in their big strong boots. Although I seldom saw a newspaper, I knew about the assassination of the Archduke Ferdinand at Sarajevo. News placards screamed out at every corner, and military bands blared out their martial music in the main streets of Croydon. This was too much for me to resist, and as if drawn by a magnet, I knew I had to enlist straight away.

From George Coppard, *With a Machine Gun to Cambrai*, published in 1969.

● **SOURCE H**

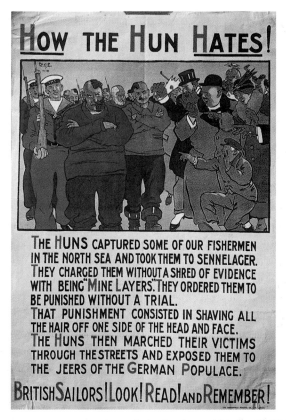

A poster issued by the British Government.

● **SOURCE I**

A photograph of a crowd in London attacking a German-owned shop in 1915.

● **SOURCE J**

A poster issued in 1917.

● **SOURCE K**

DEFENCE OF THE REALM. E.P. 6.

MINISTRY OF FOOD.

BREACHES OF THE RATIONING ORDER

The undermentioned convictions have been recently obtained:—

Court	Date	Nature of Offence	Result
HENDON	29th Aug., 1918	Unlawfully obtaining and using ration books	3 Months' Imprisonment
WEST HAM	29th Aug., 1918	Being a retailer & failing to detach proper number of coupons	Fined £20
SMETHWICK	22nd July, 1918	Obtaining meat in excess quantities	Fined £50 & £5 5s. costs
OLD STREET	4th Sept., 1918	Being a retailer selling to unregistered customer	Fined £72 & £5 5s. costs
OLD STREET	4th Sept., 1918	Not detaching sufficient coupons for meat sold	Fined £25 & £2 2s. costs
CHESTER-LE-STREET	4th Sept., 1918	Being a retailer returning number of registered customers in excess of counterfoils deposited	Fined £50 & £3 3s. costs
HIGH WYCOMBE	7th Sept., 1918	Making false statement on application for and using Ration Books unlawfully	Fined £40 & £6 4s. costs

Enforcement Branch, Local Authorities Division,
MINISTRY OF FOOD. September, 1918.

A leaflet issued by the Government in 1918.

Questions

1   Study **Sources A, B** and **C**.
    How similar are these three posters?
    Use the sources and your own knowledge to explain your answer.   [8]

2   Study **Sources D** and **E**.
    Does Source E in any way support what is being said in Source D?
    Use the sources and your own knowledge to explain your answer.   [8]

3   Study **Sources F** and **G**.
    How useful are these two sources for telling us about why men joined the army?
    Use the sources and your own knowledge to explain your answer.   [7]

4   Study **Sources H** and **I**.
    Does Source I prove that posters like Source H were successful in making people hate Germans?
    Use the sources and your own knowledge to explain your answer.   [8]

5   Study **Sources J** and **K**.
    Were these two sources issued for the same reason?
    Use the sources and your own knowledge to explain your answer.   [9]

6   Study **all** the sources.
    How far do these sources prove that government propaganda was successful?
    Use the sources and your own knowledge to explain your answer. [10]

Index

advertising 6, 7
armed forces: *see also* First World
     War
   Boer War 15
   health standards 15
   hospital units 49
   women and 31, 65
arson 40, 41
Asquith, Herbert 36, 46
   against votes for women 33, 43
   attitude to women 47, 52, 88,
     92
   replaced by Lloyd George 51

Baldwin, Stanley 94
Barnado, Dr Thomas 8
Battle of the Somme 68, 72
Battle of the Somme 71–72
Beaverbrook, Lord (William
     Maxwell Aitken) 71
Becker, Lydia 34
Besant, Annie 28
Black Friday 36, 42, 43, 44, 81
Boer War 15
bombing
   German raids 57–58
   by suffragettes 40, 41
Booth, Catherine 12
Booth, Charles 13, 15
Booth, William 12
Boswell, Percy 68
Britannia (originally *Votes for
     Women*) 49
Brooks, D C 84
'business as usual' attitude 61

Campbell-Bannerman, Sir Henry 36
cartoons
   and Liberal Government reforms
     75, 76
   of Lloyd George 78
   as propaganda 70, 71
   votes for women 29, 85, 91
Cat and Mouse Act (Prisoners,
     Temporary Discharge for
     Health, Act) 37, 38, 44
charities 8, 12
children 8, 10, 25
   education 8, 16, 22–23, 24
   health services 16, 19
   legal system and 16
Children's Act (Children's Charter)
     16
Churchill, Winston 15, 21, 63
Conciliation Bill 36–37, 40, 43
Conference on Electoral Reform
     50

conscientious objectors 55
conscription 49, 54, 59
   posters 94
Conscription Act 54
Conservative Party 15, 51
Coppard, George 94
cotton industry 7
Crooks, Will 75
Cross, C 21

Daily Chronicle 44
Daily Express 49
Daily Herald 85
Daily Mail 59
Daily Mirror 44
Dangerfield, George 82
Davison, Emily 37, 40
   suffragettes and 83–85
death 68
Degroot, G J 94
demonstrations 36, 39, 43
department stores 7
Derby, Lord 54
divorce 25, 26
dockers 13
DORA (Defence of the Realm Acts)
     59, 61
Drummond, Flora 89

education 8, 10
   free school meals 16, 19
   girls 22–23, 24
   health services 16, 19
   state schools 22
engineering industry 17, 19

family life: during First World War
     66
fashion 6, 24, 38
Fawcett, Millicent 34, 47, 49, 50,
     89
films, official   71–72
First World War 53–72
   civilians, effect on 53–58
   conscientious objectors 55
   family life 66
   food supplies, control of 60
   government propaganda 69–72
   government propaganda,
     effectiveness of 93–97
   hospital units 49
   industry, control of 59
   NUWSS and 49
   railways 59
   recruitment 49, 53–54, 55, 56,
     59, 62, 65, 86, 94
   and votes for women 89–92

women in 49, 62–67, 86–88
   WSPU and 49
food shortages 60, 66
force-feeding 36, 37, 38, 42, 43
free school meals 16, 19

*Great Scourge and How to end it,
     The* (C Pankhurst) 27, 28
Groom, W H A 94

Harrison, Mrs Frederick 32
Hay, J R 21
health services
   for children 16, 19
   provided by National Insurance
     17
health standards
   British army 15
   school medical inspections 16
housing 7, 8, 9, 74
hunger strikes 36, 37, 42, 43

industry 7
   government control of 59
   munitions 59, 63, 64, 87
   women in 63
invasion threat 58
Irish Nationalist Party 15

Jex-Blake, Sophia 25
Jones, Irving 56

Kenney, Annie 35, 89
Kitchener, Horatio Herbert, Lord 53

Labouchere, Henry 33
Labour Exchanges Act 17
Labour Party 51, 76
   formation of 15
Lancet, The 43
landgirls 49
landowners 20
Lark Rise to Candleford
     (Thompson) 77
Law, Andrew Bonar 52
Lee, Jennie 78
legal system
   treatment of children 16
   women in 25
Leigh, Mary 38
Leighton, Roland 56
leisure 7
Liberal Government reforms
     16–21, 74–79
   cartoons 75, 76
   children 16, 19
   effectiveness 19–20

historians' assessment 21
importance 77–79
National Insurance 17, 19
opposition 20
pensions 18, 19
votes for women 43
Liberal Party 15, 51, 76
suffragettes at meetings 35, 42,
43
*Life and Labour of the People in
London* (Charles Booth) 13, 15
living conditions 9, 78
Lloyd George, David 15, 21, 40
1909 budget 20
and 'business as usual' attitude
61
cartoons of 78
and food shortages 60
at Ministry of Munitions 59, 63
replaces Asquith 51
on social reforms 77, 79
and women's suffrage 47, 82
Lloyd's Weekly News 83
local government 15, 16, 19
London: poverty in 10, 12, 13
London, Jack: *People of the Abyss*
10

Manchester Society for Women's
Suffrage 34
marriage 23, 25, 26
match-makers' strike 28
McKenna, Reginald 91
medicine: women in 25, 28
meetings 39, 43, 49
middle classes
and NUWSS 34
women 25
and WPSU 35
Middlebrook, Martin 56
mining industry 59
Ministry of Food 60
Ministry of Munitions 59, 63
Ministry of Shipping 59
Mother's Day 66
Mud March 36
munitions industry 59, 63, 87
paintings 64
photographs 64
My Own Story (E Pankhurst) 35, 80

National Baby Week 66
posters 67
National Council for the
Unmarried Mother and her
Child 66
National Insurance

sickness 17, 19
unemployment 17, 19, 79
National Insurance Act (1911) 17
National Insurance Act, Part II
(1912) 17
National Registration Act 65
New Liberals 15
News of the World 45
newspapers 44, 45, 49, 59, 83, 85
and government propaganda
69
suffragette 38, 41, 42, 49, 81, 92
nursing 25
NUWSS (National Union of
Women's Suffrage Societies)
26, 29, 34, 36, 50
First World War and 49
growth in popularity 46
and middle classes 34
rise in 90
Women's Pilgrimage 37, 39, 89
and working classes 34

outdoor relief 8–9

pacifism 49
paintings 24, 64, 71
Pals' Battalions 53, 54
Pankhurst, Christabel 27, 28, 35,
37, 44, 48
*Great Scourge and How to end
it, The* 27, 28
in prison 35, 43
Unshackled 44, 48, 80, 84, 90
Pankhurst, Emmeline 26, 35, 40,
47, 63
My Own Story 35, 80
in prison 43, 44
Pankhurst, Sylvia 35, 49
The Suffrage Movement 84
pensions 18, 19, 20, 75, 77, 79
Pensions Act (1908) 18
petitions 34, 36, 40, 49
photographs 66, 95
advertising 6
bomb damage 57
education 10, 23
Emily Davison 83, 84
fashion 6
food queues 66
housing 7, 9, 74
official 71
poverty 9, 10, 11, 18
as propaganda 10, 38, 39
recruitment 54
shops 7, 95
slums 7, 74

suffragettes 28, 39, 40, 43, 80
violent protests 40, 41, 42, 95
women voting 50
women's contribution to war
49, 63, 64–65
working conditions 7, 23
Poole, Dorothy 87
Poor Law 8–9, 19, 79
popular songs 45
postcards 90
as propaganda 38, 70
posters
advertising 7
Cat and Mouse Act 38
conscription 94
food shortages 60
as government propaganda 70,
94, 95
National Baby Week 67
recruitment 53, 55, 62, 65, 94
votes for women 27, 32–33, 38
poverty 8–21: *see also* National
Insurance; pensions
causes of 9, 12, 13, 14
circles of 12
economic implications 15
in London 10, 12, 13
political implications 15
primary 14
secondary 14
In York 9, 14
Poverty: a Study of Town Life
(Rowntree) 9, 15
poverty line 13, 14
propaganda 38
cartoons 70, 71
First World War 69–72, 93–97
government 69–72, 93–97
newspapers 69
photographs 10, 38, 39
postcards 38, 70
posters 27, 32–33, 38, 70, 94, 95
suffrage movement 38
prostitution 12, 26, 27
public meetings 39, 43, 49
Pugh, Martin 82, 89, 90, 91
Punch 70, 76

railways 7
during First World War 59
rationing 60–61
recruitment
conscription 49, 54, 59, 94
posters 53, 55, 62, 65, 94
volunteers 53–54, 56, 94
of women 65
Reeves, Maud Pember 74

Reform Bill (1911) 37
Regulation 40D 67
Rent Registration Act 66
rent strikes 66
retirement 9, 18
Roberts, Richard 77
Rosen, Andrew 48
Rowntree, Benjamin Seebohm 9, 14, 15
    Poverty: a Study of Town Life 9, 15

Salvation Army 10, 12
sanitation 8, 15
Saunders, Robert 58
school clinics 16
school medical inspections 16
separate spheres 28, 30
separation allowances 66
shelling campaigns 57–58
shipping industry 17, 19, 59
shops 7, 23, 38, 95
sickness 9
    and National Insurance 17, 19
Sims, George: *Living London* 10
slums 7, 8, 74
social reforms *see* Liberal
    Government reforms
soup kitchens 10, 12
STDs (sexually transmitted
    diseases) 27, 28, 67
Steavenson, Archie 57
Stevenson, Frances 71
street cleaning 15
street lighting 15
strikes
    hunger 36, 37, 42, 43
    match-makers 28
    rent 66
Suffrage Movement, The (S
    Pankhurst) 84
Suffragette, The 41, 49
suffragettes 34, 44–45
    attacks on people 42
    attacks on property 40–41
    and Emily Davison 83–85
    force-feeding 36, 37, 38, 42, 43
    hunger strikes 36, 37, 42, 43
    meetings and demonstrations 36, 39, 43
    peaceful protests 38–40
    petitions 40
    photographs 28, 39, 40, 43, 80
    propaganda 38
    violence, attitudes to 89
    violence, justification for 80–82
    violent protests 35, 36–37, 40–42

violent protests, assessment of 46
suffragists 34, 36–37
    meetings and demonstrations 39
    peaceful protests 38–40
    petitions 34, 36, 40, 49
    propaganda 38

taxation 20, 40
teaching 25, 28
Thompson, Flora: *Lark Rise to Candleford* 77
Times, The 44, 45, 69, 81, 84, 89
    letters 20, 78
trade unions 87
    attitude to women 51, 63

unemployment 8, 13
    and National Insurance 17, 19, 79
universities: women in 25, 28
Unshackled (C Pankhurst) 44, 48, 80, 84, 90
upper classes 6
    women 24
    and WPSU 35

venereal disease 27, 28
Victoria, Queen 8
violence
    assessment of 46
suffragettes and 35, 36, 37, 40–42, 80–82, 89
votes for men 8, 29, 37, 50
votes for women 22–52, 89–92
    arguments against 30–31, 33, 43
    arguments for 26–29
    cartoons 29, 85, 91
    First World War and 89–92
    Liberal Government and 43
    newspapers, attitude of 44
    partial suffrage granted 50–51
    peaceful protests 38–40
    petitions 34, 36, 40, 49
    posters 27, 32–33, 38
    violent protests 35, 36–37, 40–42
Votes for Women 38, 42, 81, 91
    renamed *Britannia* 49
voting figures: early 20th century 76

wages 8, 13, 59
    comparisons 23, 25, 63
water supplies 8, 15
Williams, Joan 87

window-smashing 36, 40, 80
Woman's Weekly problem page 88
women *see also* votes for women
    and armed forces 31, 65
    banned from Liberal Party meetings 42, 43
    divorce 25, 26
    employment 23, 25, 49, 62–65
    expectations 6
    in First World War 49, 62–67, 86–88
    inequality with men 23, 25, 26
    in legal profession 25
    marriage 23, 25, 26
    in medicine 25, 28
    middle classes 25
    motherhood encouraged 66
    in politics 28
    in teaching 25, 28
    trade unions and 51, 63
    in universities 25, 28
    upper classes 24
    Victorian view 22
    working classes 22, 23, 51
Women's Land Army 63, 65
Women's Party (formerly WSPU) 49
Women's Pilgrimage (NUWSS, 1913) 37, 39, 89
Women's Right to Serve rally 49, 63
workhouses 8, 9, 75, 79
    Cambridge 11
working classes 6
    and NUWSS 34
    and WPSU 35
    women 22, 23, 51
working conditions 7, 8, 23
WSPU (Women's Social and Political Union) 26, 27, 34, 35, 36–37, 89
    badges and brooches 38
    decline of 46, 48, 90
    and First World War 49
    imprisonment 35, 36
    and middle classes 35
    posters 27, 32–33
    renamed Women's Party 49
    and upper classes 35
    violent protests 35, 36
    Votes for Women 38, 42, 49, 81, 91
    and working classes 35

York: poverty in 9, 14

Zeppelins 57, 58